"I have lost count of the [...]
Priceless wisdom and exquisite summaries of Old Testament
genres, with the added bonus of Motyer's wit and wisdom, make
this book a treasure indeed."

Derek W. H. Thomas, Senior Minister, First Presbyterian
Church, Columbia, South Carolina; Chancellor's Professor
of Systematic and Pastoral Theology, Reformed Theological
Seminary; Teaching Fellow, Ligonier Ministries

"Alec Motyer was both a princely man and a prince among Old
Testament theologians, teachers, and authors. Devout and witty,
scholarly and accessible, theological and commonsensical, God-
honoring and Christ-centered, Spirit-illuminated and practical—
he seemed to sprinkle gold dust on every page he wrote. And from
seminary-trained leaders to the youngest believer, every reader can
share his generosity by a little digging into 6 *Ways the Old Testament Speaks Today.*"

Sinclair B. Ferguson, Chancellor's Professor of Systematic
Theology, Reformed Theological Seminary; Teaching Fellow,
Ligonier Ministries

6 WAYS THE OLD TESTAMENT SPEAKS TODAY

6 WAYS THE OLD TESTAMENT SPEAKS TODAY

An Interactive Guide

Alec Motyer

CROSSWAY®

WHEATON, ILLINOIS

6 *Ways the Old Testament Speaks Today: An Interactive Guide*

© Alec Motyer 1994, 2016

Published by Crossway
        1300 Crescent Street
        Wheaton, Illinois 60187

Originally published as *A Scenic Route through the Old Testament* by Inter-Varsity Press, London, England, 1994 (first edition), 2016 (second edition). North American edition published in 2018 by permission of Inter-Varsity Press.

Cover design: Darren Welch Design

Cover image: Moses with the Tablets of the Law (oil on canvas), Guido Reni (1575–1642) / Bridgeman Images

First North American printing 2018

Printed in the United States of America

Unless otherwise indicated, Scripture quotations are from the ESV® Bible (The Holy Bible, English Standard Version®), copyright © 2001 by Crossway, a publishing ministry of Good News Publishers. Used by permission. All rights reserved.

Scripture quotations marked KJV are from the *King James Version* of the Bible.

Scripture references marked NIV are taken from The Holy Bible, New International Version®, NIV®. Copyright © 1973, 1978, 1984, 2011 by Biblica, Inc.™ Used by permission. All rights reserved worldwide.

Scripture references marked NKJV are from *The New King James Version*. Copyright © 1982, Thomas Nelson, Inc. Used by permission.

Scripture references marked NRSV are from *The New Revised Standard Version*. Copyright © 1989 by the Division of Christian Education of the National Council of the Churches of Christ in the USA. Published by Thomas Nelson, Inc. Used by permission of the National Council of the Churches of Christ in the USA.

All emphases in Scripture quotations have been added by the author.

Trade paperback ISBN: 978-1-4335-5851-1
ePub ISBN: 978-1-4335-5854-2
PDF ISBN: 978-1-4335-5852-8
Mobipocket ISBN: 978-1-4335-5853-5

Library of Congress Cataloging-in-Publication Data

Names: Motyer, J. A., author.
Title: 6 ways the Old Testament speaks today : an interactive guide / Alec Motyer.
Other titles: Six ways the Old Testament speaks today
Description: Wheaton : Crossway, 2018. | Includes bibliographical references and index.
Identifiers: LCCN 2017022966 (print) | LCCN 2018005409 (ebook) | ISBN 9781433558528 (pdf) | ISBN 9781433558535 (mobi) | ISBN 9781433558542 (epub) | ISBN 9781433558511 (tp)
Subjects: LCSH: Bible. Old Testament—Criticism, interpretation, etc.
Classification: LCC BS1171.3 (ebook) | LCC BS1171.3 .M68 2018 (print) | DDC 221.6—dc23
LC record available at https://lccn.loc.gov/2017022966

Crossway is a publishing ministry of Good News Publishers.

VP   27   26   25   24   23   22   21   20   19   18
15   14   13   12   11   10   9   8   7   6   5   4   3   2   1

CONTENTS

PREFACE TO THE SECOND EDITION

My father died in August 2016, just when a new edition of his *Scenic Route through the Old Testament*, which is being published by Crossway in this edition as *6 Ways the Old Testament Speaks Today*, had gotten to the "first page-proof" stage. It was my delight and privilege to help it over the last steps to publication and to rejoice again in his deep love for Scripture, his intense desire to encourage others in regular Bible reading, and his amazing gift for hearing Scripture exactly and explaining it clearly.

For this new edition, he added a week's worth of daily guided readings to each chapter. In addition, each chapter has a month of daily readings in the appendix. I know he would tell us to focus on the readings and dispense with his chapter! But the chapters are of such good value, and it is great to see them brought to life again in this new edition. My father still speaks, even though now united with his Lord in glory. We thank God for him.

Steve Motyer
Watford, Hertfordshire

PREFACE TO THE FIRST EDITION

In the first half of 1989, while I was vicar of Christ Church Westbourne, the Adult Education Committee of the Bournemouth Deanery (the local grouping of Church of England churches) invited me to give a series of lectures on the Old Testament. I owe a big debt of gratitude to Keith Rawlings, who "fathered" the enterprise, and to the resolute company who braved winter nights and made the whole series so memorable and happy for me.

This was the early proving ground for five of the six chapters of this book, with their associated schemes of Bible reading. I have added the chapter and readings on wisdom for the sake of completeness.

As I see it, the scheme of readings and notes is much more important than the introductory chapters. The Bible is just what the advertisers used to claim for Bisto gravy (for those of you who remember the advertisement)—as soon as the aroma wafts their way, the Bisto kids lift their noses to it and head for home! When we settle down to reading the Bible, we soon catch the scent, and the Bible's Lord himself will be our teacher.

This is not to say that the chapters are unimportant. It is in them that the panorama of the Old Testament scene is spread out. They are meant to be lookout points. Read them with Bible in hand and look up the references that are given. But should you find them unduly hard going, get on with the readings and return to the chapters later.

May the Lord richly bless you as you come with me for a country walk through the first and larger part of his Word.

Alec Motyer
Bishopsteignton, Devon

INTRODUCTION

Do you find the Old Testament more than a little bit daunting? Don't worry, you are not alone. Many, many people do. And really, it's no wonder. The first part of our Bibles is a large book; it often seems remote from our present-day needs and ways; not all its material is easy to grasp; it even gives the impression of lots of wars; and when we come to grips with its main characters, we find rascals among the saints. Besides all this, the real question arises: why bother about the Old when we are the people of the New?

But all those first impressions give the wrong idea. The Old Testament is not really like that at all. Actually, it is a rather spectacular piece of countryside, full of interest, and (wonderfully) speaking directly to us, our situations, and our needs. Did you ever notice a striking thing Stephen said in his speech in Acts 7:38, that Moses "received living oracles to give to us"—the vital Word of God itself relevant to each successive generation right up to "us"? Paul insisted on the same truth in Romans 15:4: "For whatever was written in former days was written for our instruction."

And when we turn to the highest authority of all, the Lord Jesus Christ, what do we find? Well, if we had asked him, "Why do you keep quoting the Old Testament?" he would have replied, "The Old what?" And when we explained, he would have corrected us: "You mean 'the word of God' (Mark 7:13), 'the Scriptures' (John 5:39)"—nothing "old" about that as far as Jesus was concerned, for it is actually the applicable truth of God by which he was content to plan his life and accept his cross (Matt. 26:53–54). The big word he used was "the Law" (Luke 10:26), a word that actually means "the Teaching," the living directions of a caring parent to a beloved child ("instruction," Prov. 4:1)— in the case of our Lord, his heavenly Father's voice in his ear. Should we not prize—and go all out to understand—what was so precious to our Savior?

This book tries to give you a taste of six main Old Testament themes—history, religion, worship, prophecy, wisdom, and theology (the revelation of God)—and it does so by means of six introductory chapters, backed up by daily readings from appropriate passages. I am grateful to Mrs. Kate Byrom, formerly at IVP, for the suggestion of how to make the book more user-friendly. In consequence, each chapter now has six days of readings with brief notes, while the original months of readings linked with each chapter have now been moved to an appendix for those who want to take matters further.

In my opinion the readings are more important than the introductions, so if you find any chapter best left for later, why not get on with the readings and then come back to it?

In what we must still call "the Old Testament," the past speaks to the present. If God be pleased, you will find his marvelous Word speaking to you day by day for your rich blessing and constant encouragement.

1

THE VOICE OF HISTORY

A Review

Between the time when the Lord called Abraham (Genesis 12) and the time of Malachi, the last of the prophets, there are about 1,500 years. Within this time span the Old Testament tells how the Lord chose one man, gave him a family, and made the family into a nation. Patiently he persevered with that nation through thick and thin, never deviating from his freely given commitment to be their God.

Figure 1.1 (p. 16) shows an outline of the story. A chart can only give an impression: this is what the skeleton of Old Testament history looks like. But put some flesh on the bare bones by following the events on the map on page 17 (see fig. 1.2).

One Man to Bless the World

God had a worldwide purpose when he called Abram from Ur of the Chaldeans (Gen. 11:31–12:5; 15:7), and we, marveling at the simple trust of the man who "went out, not knowing where he was going" (Heb. 11:8), can follow him along the established trade route from Ur to Haran and on into Canaan. He went on his way trusting the promises God had made to him—that he would be a universal blessing (Gen. 12:2–3) and possess the land of Canaan (15:7). In due course the promises passed to Isaac (17:19–21) and then to Jacob (27:27–29; 28:13–15).

Topic	References	Dates
The Family	Genesis	2000–1500 BC
Abraham	Genesis 12–25	
Isaac	Genesis 21–35	
Jacob and his twelve sons	Genesis 25–50	
The Nation	Exodus–Ruth	1400–1100 BC
Moses and the exodus	Exodus–Deuteronomy	
Joshua and the conquest	Joshua	
Early life in Canaan	Judges–Ruth	
The Monarchy		1100–586 BC
The united kingdom		1050–930 BC
Saul	1 Samuel	1050–1000 BC
David	1 Samuel 16–1 Kings 2	1000–960 BC
	1 Chronicles 10–29	
Solomon	1 Kings 1–11	960–930 BC
	2 Chronicles 1–9	
The two kingdoms	1 Kings 12	
The kings of Israel	1 Kings 12–2 Kings 17	930–722 BC
The kings of Judah	1 Kings 12–2 Kings 25	930–586 BC
	2 Chronicles 10–36	
The Exile		
Babylon	2 Kings 25	586–540 BC
The Return	Ezra–Nehemiah	539 BC

Figure 1.1   Story outline of the Old Testament

Possessing the Land

Part of the promise was fulfilled when Jacob's sons, now a large nation (Ex. 1:1–7), left Egypt under Moses and later entered and possessed Canaan under Joshua. The book of Joshua tells how the land was conquered (see Josh. 1:1–5; 21:43–45). Judges 1 sketches how individual tribes claimed their inheritance, but the main message of Judges is the good care of the Lord in providing judge-deliverers according to the people's need but contrary to their deserving (2:10–19).

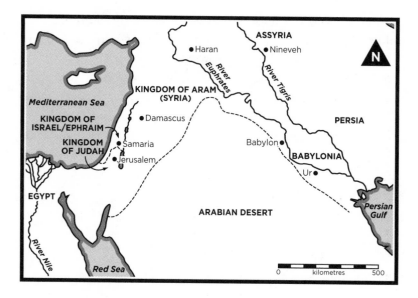

Figure 1.2   Map of the ancient Near East

The Kings

Then the people asked for a king (1 Sam. 8:6), and after the failure of Saul's kingship (1 Sam. 8:1–7; 10:20–24; 13:13–14; 15:26), David united the kingdom around his new capital city, Jerusalem (2 Sam. 5:6–9). His son Solomon further cemented this unity by building in Jerusalem a temple, or dwelling place, for the Lord (1 Kings 6:1, 37–38).

But Solomon's son Rehoboam was the sort of person we would today call a "loser." Under his reign, the kingdom broke into two (1 Kings 12:1–19), with Israel (also called Jacob and Ephraim) to the north and Judah to the south.

Exile and Return

The single dynasty of David lasted in Jerusalem for four hundred years, but in the north one dynasty followed another. King succeeded king by conquest and assassination until Israel was taken captive to Assyria in 722 BC. Judah, however, did not fall to Assyria's imperial successor, Babylon, until 586 BC, and then the exile of the Lord's people was complete. But the faithful Lord never allows his promises to lapse (Ezra 1:1). He brought them home again in 539 BC but only to live as provincial subjects within the Persian Empire. They were never again a sovereign, independent state, and the dynasty of David was not to surface again until he came whose right it is to reign (Luke 1:29–33).

What Sort of History?

There are five things we can say about Old Testament history.

Old Testament History Is Reliable

Specialist opinion regarding Old Testament history has undergone a wide pendulum swing. There was a time when specialists were saying that the stories should be accepted as true only if verified by evidence from outside the Old Testament. But now many are prepared to allow that the stories can be assumed to be true unless other evidence contradicts them. It is fair to say that the major tendency of outside evidence is to confirm what we read in the Bible. But we have a much surer foundation to rest on than this piece of evidence or that. Our great privilege is to look beyond specialist opinion to the Lord Jesus Christ. When he referred to stories in the Old Testament, it is plain that he accepted them as the wholly reliable Word of God, and we who follow him need have no hesitation in accepting as true whatever the Old Testament is found to affirm about events and their sequence.

The words "found to affirm" are important. Old Testament history is not problem-free. It is not easy, for example, to fit together the reigns of the kings of Israel and Judah from dates and chronologies supplied by the books of Kings; neither is it certain who is referred to as "Darius the Mede" in Daniel 5:31. On the other hand, it is clear from archaeology that the stories of Abraham, Isaac, Jacob, and Joseph accurately reflect life and customs in the period 2000–1500 BC. Details formerly disputed (like the very existence of Belshazzar, Daniel 5) are now well established. We need to work at the stories until we are sure what it is the Old Testament is saying and claiming.

Old Testament History Is Selective

In being selective, Old Testament history is no different from every attempt to write history. Not even the longest history book, inside or outside the Bible, contains all that happened in its chosen period. H. A. L. Fisher wrote his *History of Europe* without making any reference to my grandmother. The same is true of R. F. Foster in his book *Modern Ireland 1600–1972*, even though the old lady lived in Ireland well within this period. Were I to write of the years 1850–1939, Grandma would figure very largely indeed. It is all a matter of what a writer thinks important.

Even historians who cannot discern any purpose in the flow of history still have to decide what to include and what to leave out. This is just as true of the Old Testament, not because it contains a peculiar sort of history or because its writers were ignorant or biased but because selection is the only way to write history.

Take Manasseh as an example. He reigned for many years over Judah (ca. 690–640 BC), and economically, politically, and militarily, he was an astute ruler, but 2 Kings tells us nothing of all this. Only eighteen verses are allotted to his fifty-five years (2 Kings 21:1–18), and they say, in effect, only one thing about Manasseh: "He did what was evil in the sight of the LORD" (v. 2).

Fifty-five years and only one fact! It would be easy to dismiss such history writing as no history at all. How very different it is from modern histories with their social, economic, political, and military detail. But notice verse 17:

> Now the rest of the acts of Manasseh and all that he did, . . .
> are they not written in the Book of the Chronicles of the Kings
> of Judah?

In other words, the Old Testament historian had all the facts available, but he simply did not think them important for his purpose. Rather, this was his concern:

> Still the LORD did not turn from the burning of his great wrath
> . . . against Judah, because of all the provocations with which
> Manasseh had provoked him. And the LORD said, "I will re-
> move Judah . . . , and I will cast off this city that I have chosen,
> Jerusalem." (2 Kings 23:26)

The point is that it was Manasseh's moral and spiritual failure that subsequently caused the ruin of Judah and Jerusalem. In 2 Kings 23:26, notice the word "still." Manasseh was succeeded by Josiah (2 Kings 22–23). Unlike his father, Josiah was devoted to the Lord. Indeed, of all the kings of Judah he came nearest to the ideal, the "golden boy," David. Think of it this way: Manasseh dropped a huge brick into the pond; Josiah, by his godliness and his reforms, fetched the brick out again, but nothing could stop the ripples that Manasseh had set in motion.

Why then should we need to know of Manasseh's domestic and foreign policies? It was not on them that history turned, for it is righteousness, not astuteness, that exalts a nation (Prov. 14:34). All Old Testament history is selectively written to demonstrate this single principle. The fortunes of nations are settled not by economic, political, military, or diplomatic factors but by their standing before God.

Old Testament History Is God-Centered

The Hebrew Bible—the Old Testament—consists of three sections. They are arranged differently from our English versions (which follow the order given in the Septuagint, the Greek translation of the Old Testament) and are grouped as shown in figure 1.3.

The Law
Genesis, Exodus, Leviticus, Numbers, Deuteronomy

The Prophets
a. The Former Prophets: Joshua, Judges, Samuel, Kings
b. The Latter Prophets: Isaiah, Jeremiah, Ezekiel, Hosea, Joel, Amos, Obadiah, Jonah, Micah, Nahum, Habakkuk, Zephaniah, Haggai, Zechariah, Malachi

The Writings
a. Psalms, Job, Proverbs
b. Song of Songs, Ruth, Lamentations, Ecclesiastes, Esther
c. Daniel, Ezra, Nehemiah, Chronicles

Figure 1.3   Arrangement of the Hebrew Bible

This is the Bible as Jesus knew it. In the upper room on the first Easter Day, he spoke to his disciples about how "everything written about me in the Law of Moses and the Prophets and the Psalms must be fulfilled" (Luke 24:44). It is pretty marvelous to realize that we have the same Bible the Lord Jesus knew and loved.

But the particular point to notice is that the early editors, who organized the Bible books into the three-section order of the Hebrew Bible, described the history books of Samuel and Kings as "prophets." How can this be? What does it mean?

When we speak of "prophets," we often mean "predictors" or "forecasters," but this is only one of the things a prophet did. Acts 2:11 and 17 will help us here. As the crowd listened to the apostles speaking on the day of Pentecost, Peter reminded them that Joel had predicted that "your sons and your daughters shall prophesy." However, what the listeners heard them proclaiming was not predictions but "the mighty works of God." This is how the Old Testament history books are prophecy: they are written in order to tell us about God and the way he runs the world; they are a record of his wonderful works.

Listen to Amos:

Did I not bring up Israel from the land of Egypt,
    And the Philistines from Caphtor and the Syrians from Kir?
        (Amos 9:7)

This must have been a shock to Amos's listeners. They had been raised to believe that their God's "mighty works" in bringing them out from Egyptian slavery were unique to them. This was right as far as it went. Sadly, however, they had come to think of the exodus simply as a date on the calendar and of themselves as right with God simply because that date had passed. Nothing could be more false or misleading. The fact is that the mere presence of a date on the calendar—whether Christmas, Easter, or any other event—saves no one.

So Amos was challenging a deadly spiritual complacency that said, "We must be right with God because the exodus happened," irrespective of personal trust or obedience or holiness. He challenged it head-on: "As far as the exodus is concerned, why, you are no different from anyone else! Who do you think masterminded the migration of the Philistines from Caphtor and of the Arameans from Kir? You boast of your exodus, but your God is so great that he is behind every movement of peoples and nations!" He is the God of *all* history.

Listen to Isaiah:

Woe to Assyria, the rod of my anger;
    the staff in their hands is my fury!
Against a godless nation I send him . . .
to take spoil and seize plunder. . . .
But he does not so intend, . . .
but it is in his heart to destroy,
    and to cut off nations not a few. . . .

When the Lord has finished all his work on Mount Zion and on Jerusalem, he will punish the speech of the arrogant heart of the king of Assyria and the boastful look in his eyes.

Shall the axe boast over him who hews with it,
  or the saw magnify itself against him who wields it?
    (Isa. 10:5–7, 12, 15)

Assyria was the superpower of the day. We must not belittle that power simply because their weapons seem so primitive compared with the savage weapons of destruction that are the childish pride of nations today. The Assyrians had developed the most advanced war machine of their time; they were dreaded for their seemingly invincible capacity for total war. However, says Isaiah, what is Assyria but an expression of the Lord's wrath (v. 5), a messenger on the Lord's errand (v. 6), and a tool in the Lord's hand (v. 15)? The superpower on earth and the superior power of a sovereign God!

One major lesson of all the history books, and one reason why so much of the Old Testament is occupied with history, is that we may see that behind all events and behind their whole sequence is a great and wonderful God engineering and controlling everything and working his purposes out in the flow of history.

Old Testament History Is Moral

Let's stay with Isaiah 10:5–15. Assyria invaded Judah and threatened Jerusalem in 701 BC. It was a justly deserved disaster for the Judahites, and Assyria was the Lord's chastising rod. But from the point of view of the king of Assyria, nothing of the sort was happening. He was an imperialist. He took it for granted that it was his right to rule the world, that if he so wished he would jolly well do so, and that Jerusalem was as helplessly and rightfully his prey as all the other nations he had conquered (vv. 7–11). He was wholly motivated by what Isaiah calls his "arrogant heart" (v. 12). Under a sovereign God, Assyria's power would be used for the Lord's holy purposes (vv. 6, 12); under a holy God, Assyria's pride would be punished (vv. 12–15).

The king of Assyria was both a tool in the Lord's hand and a responsible agent in his own right. Isaiah helps us to understand this a little by suggesting an illustration:

> Because you have raged against me
> > and your complacency has come to my ears,
> I will put my hook in your nose
> > and my bit in your mouth,
> and I will turn you back on the way
> > by which you came. (Isa. 37:29)

The Assyrian king was like a powerful horse with enormous energy and drive, but the Lord was the rider determining where and to what extent that power could be used. In this way the Bible reveals a God who is not only fully sovereign but also undeviatingly holy. It also reveals a world in which people are fully responsible for what they do and yet live within the control of divine rule.

Many are troubled by the fact that the Old Testament seems so full of war and cruelty: "Such a savage book," people say.

There are three things to be said about this. First, we must be careful not to criticize the Old Testament for being realistic. Its history, after all, is about this world, and if it contained no wars with their cruelties, probably the same people who accuse it of savagery would be the first to criticize it for living in a dream world.

Second, the Old Testament does not necessarily approve of all it records. Its stories rarely embody a moral comment one way or the other; we are usually left to draw our own conclusions of right or wrong. Consequently, actually to be told in 2 Samuel 11:27 that "the thing that David had done displeased the Lord" is somewhat out of the ordinary.

Another incident in the life of David is allowed to pass without comment. The Lord brought David to the throne without his fighting for it. He promised it to David and kept his promises (2 Sam. 7:8–11). Equally, David, for his part, resolutely refused to seize the throne for himself (1 Sam. 24:4–7; 26:8–11). Once he was on the throne, however, what do we find? He went to war against the poor rump of Saul's kingdom ruled by the incompetent and rather pathetic Ish-Bosheth (2 Sam. 2:8–4:12). By doing so, he sowed seeds of bloodshed that would in due course become a harvest of hatred and division.

Was this war justified? Should not David have continued to trust that the Lord who had kept his promises so far would go on keeping promises until they were all fulfilled? Does the Old Testament approve of this war making? Surely not! It is recorded not because the Old Testament delights in war but because its people (even the best of them) are tragically human and their lives blighted by human frailties.

In other words, the history books of the Old Testament not only reveal God but also reveal people. Even the best of them were sinful—lustful, ambitious, cruel, mistaken. Like us, they failed, and their failures are faithfully recorded in this most honest of books. Indeed, isn't it one of the greatest of the "mighty works of God" that he continues to bother with such people?

Third, the long sweep of Old Testament history allows us to see the holy God governing the world by his own moral laws. Joshua entered Canaan with a mandate that horrifies us: he was to put to death every human being without regard to age or sex (e.g., Josh. 6:21). But this frightfulness is the end of a long story that began in Genesis 15:16. The time was four hundred years earlier, and the Lord was speaking to Abraham:

And they shall come back here in the fourth generation, for the iniquity of the Amorites is not yet complete.

Even on a timescale of centuries, history is governed by the Lord's moral rules. To take the land of the Amorites from them and give it to Abraham just like that would have been an injustice. They were its rightful owners, and their rights had to be respected. But in four hundred years' time, the story would be different. They would have had four centuries of probation, and by the end of that time their "iniquity" would have been "complete." Awful as would be their end, it was no more than the wages of their sin (Rom. 6:23). "Shall not the Judge of all the earth do what is just?" (Gen. 18:25).

Old Testament History Is a Record of Failure

The people asked for a king (1 Sam. 8:5; 12:12) because they thought that an organized monarchy would be the end of all their troubles. It would have been, if only they had been able to find a king equal to the task.

In the southern kingdom of Judah, the descendants of David sat on his throne in ordered succession. David was the Lord's own king; he and his sons sat on what is called "the throne of the Lord" (1 Chron. 29:23). Yet their kingdom failed, and to the human eye, the dynasty petered out.

The northern kingdom of Israel was ruled by monarchs who came to the throne by natural gifts of leadership and in pursuit of personal ambition. Although one dynasty after another did the best that human ability could achieve, this kingdom too failed and disappeared.

In this way, Old Testament history is one long cry for something better, for a true king who would satisfy his people's aspirations for peace and safety, reigning in perfection and ruling in righteousness. Like every other "voice" in the Old Testament, the voice of history is a prayer for the coming of the Messiah.

BIBLE READINGS
Old Testament History

Day 1: Where It All Began (Gen. 2:4–24)

Start with verse 4 and look at what the ESV phrases "the generations of" (NIV: "the account of"). This formula occurs eleven times in Genesis,[1] always with the same meaning. The noun comes from

---

1. See Gen. 5:1; 6:9; 10:1; 11:10, 27; 25:12, 19; 36:1, 9; 37:2.

the verb "to beget" or "to bring forth," and it strictly means "that which emerges from," or "what comes." In short, it introduces not just "the account" but "the continuing story." So Genesis 2:4–24 is not (as many say) a second account of creation but rather what emerged out of the majestic account of creation in 1:1–2:3. And as we see, "what happened next," or "what emerged," was the beginnings of human history on earth. Note how the narrative falls into two parts: in the account of creation, days one through three form the environment, and days four through six fill it with life. So here in chapter 2, verses 4–17 tell of the forming of the arena, the garden, and end with the law for life in the garden (v. 17), while verses 18–24 dwell on animal and human life and end with the law of marriage (v. 24).

In its apparently simple way, this beautiful description of how and where it all began contains a truth that is going to prove central to all the history writing in the Bible: obedience to God's Word is the key to blessing and fullness of life; disobedience brings disaster and loss of blessedness. It's so obvious, isn't it? Adam and Eve have all that a generous, openhanded God can give them (v. 16), and to remain in benefit and enjoyment, all they have to do is obey the one simple law of the garden: to not eat of the tree of the knowledge of good and evil (v. 17). The law is neither complicated nor elaborate. One sole commandment—and as long as they keep it, the whole garden with all its bounty is theirs. How easy is that! How typical of the One whom we will soon know as "the God of all grace" to make so much richness available at such negligible cost.

Think for a moment about the marriage law too. Marriage demands (as the older translations say) "leaving" and "cleaving": the replacement of old loyalty (parents) with a new, supreme loyalty (husband to wife, wife to husband) and a commitment to life-long oneness and mutuality—none of it either hard or unwelcome in the light of Adam's delighted cry of greeting at the first sight of his wife (v. 23). In Hebrew he is *ish* ("man"), and she is *ishshah* (his counterpart, "woman").

Put it all together then. Human history is planned and given by the Lord God; the clue to life in God's story is to obey his Word.

Day 2: Disaster and Promise (Gen. 3:1–24)

Our sense of sin is so inadequate and our awareness of the seriousness of sinfulness so diminished that it is hard to resist the temptation to think that the Lord God has gone somewhat over the top in his reaction to what was (after all) "only" eating from a forbidden tree. But think: first of all, although it was a simple prohibition—elementary even—it was not a tiny fault but a breach of *the whole law of God*, a contradiction of all that God required. Now look at Genesis 3:6:

- "good for food, . . . a delight to the eyes": Already the human emotions are running counter to the will of God, desiring what he has forbidden.
- "desired to make one wise": This is the mind (and logic) of humankind contradicting the mind of God, for God said, "In the day that you eat of it you shall surely die" (2:17), but man is saying, "But it is called the tree of the knowledge of good and evil," so (obviously) it will impart knowledge and wisdom.
- "she took of its fruit": The human will has made its decision.

And that is in fact the totality of human nature: emotions, mind, and will. There's nothing more. In a word, then, in Eden, the whole law of God was flouted by the whole of human nature. This was no ordinary sin, nor was it a minor offense. It was sin to the uttermost, sin at its most outrageous and sinful.

Now trace the consequences of this primal sin as Genesis outlines them. First, there is the destruction of marriage as God intended it: loss of innocence (3:7), of husbandly care and consideration (v. 12); domination replacing responsive love (v. 16); the woman named for her function instead of for her coequal partnership (v. 20). Then there is a dislocation of the environment ("thorns and thistles," v. 18) and the spontaneous bounty of the garden replaced by a lifelong toil to extract a living from a recalcitrant earth (v. 19)—in other words, sin vitiates the economic basis of life on earth (what are today called "market forces"). And of course, there is a banishment and debarring from the garden (v. 24). We may also wonder if Eve's pains in childbearing were increased by the knowledge that her sin would infect each and every succeeding generation and individual. Why? All because of the fundamental error of disobedience (v. 17).

But the story is not quite over yet. It is right to see verse 15 as the first messianic prediction in the Bible, indeed, to ask whatever else could it be. The satanic architect of all our woes will be crushed to death, the huge attempt at usurping divine rule will be brought to an end, the Victor will accept and endure the cost of this conflict undertaken for our liberation, and the glad, glad day will come when we will know "the woman" to be Mary and will exult in the triumph of Jesus Christ our Lord.

Day 3: God with Us (Ex. 3:1–8; 6:1–8; 29:42–45)

Nothing introduces us to the unexplained mysteries of life quite so well as Old Testament history. Why was Israel sent down to Egypt (Gen. 46:3)? Why were four generations of slavery divinely decreed? "History" is always "His Story." In today's readings we explore ways in which the Lord actually makes the puzzling (to them, not to him) experiences of life his story alongside his people.

He Identifies with Us in Our Needs and Hardships (Ex. 3:1–8)

We can make a few observations about the way God identifies with us in our difficulties.

1. He comes to us as the eternally living God (Ex. 3:2). "Fire," of course, always speaks of the unapproachable—even

dangerous—active holiness of God (more later), but what Moses saw was a self-perpetuating flame that needed no fuel to feed on to keep it alight: "The bush is not burned" (v. 3; cf. Rev. 1:18). Think of the force of that truth coming to a people under sentence of death (Ex. 1:16) and gripped in slavery by the superpower of the day.

2. The Holy One makes it an easy thing for us to live right in the presence of his holiness (Ex. 3:5). Typical of all his dealing with us comes the incredible simplicity of "take your sandals off your feet." It underlines the (equally incredible) truth that the living God actually desires us to come to him, to stand in his presence. So he raises the understandably prostrate Ezekiel and sets him on his feet (Ezek. 1:28–2:2). And think of the ease of access we enjoy, right into the Most Holy Place through the blood of Jesus (Heb. 10:19–22).

3. The Holy One hears, knows, and himself identifies with us. Observe the sequence in Exodus 3:7–8: "seen the affliction . . . heard their cry . . . know their sufferings [lit., 'know their sorrows'] . . . come down to deliver."

Yahweh Redeems (Ex. 6:1–8)

Moses made a colossal mess of his first interview with Pharaoh (contrast what he was told to do and say in Ex. 4:21 with what he did and said in 5:1). Consequently, he had to complain that nothing had been achieved except more trouble (5:22–23). Yahweh has not yet started! He interjects a magnificent "now" (6:1). In his declaration of intent, he begins and ends (6:2, 8) by announcing his divine name. The coming action is going to be a revelation of Yahweh. For this reason the new element in the words is vitally significant. Most of verses 2–8 repeat what we know already, but verse 6 adds, "I will redeem you with an outstretched arm." The "arm" stands for a person taking personal interventional action with all his strength. The verb "to redeem" points to a unique Old Testament institution—that of the next of kin whose right it is to come to his needy relative and, in effect, say, "Whatever your trouble is, give it to me; I will make it mine and deal with it for you." So in Egypt the great Next of kin came alongside his firstborn son (4:22) and took on himself the whole burden of Egyptian bondage, genocide, helplessness, hopelessness, and the need for liberation, and both made it his own and undertook to deal with it.

The Indwelling God (Ex. 29:42–46)

Pretty much the whole of the end of Exodus focuses on the plans for the tabernacle (chaps. 25–31) and the building of the tabernacle (chaps. 35–40). So why is it so important? Because it is Yahweh's tent, to be pitched at the heart of his people's camp, "that I might dwell among them"—and this, insists 29:45–46, was the whole point of bringing them out of Egypt, the great objective of the Next of kin in his work of redemption.

Day 4: The Way "History" Works (Judg. 2:11–22)

What we find in the short passage of Judges 2:11–22 can be traced right through the history books of the Old Testament. There is a rhythm that holds history together (vv. 11–15). The verbs sum it up: "did what was evil . . . served the Baals . . . provoked . . . abandoned." And all this had a consequence: "sold . . . no longer withstand . . . harm . . . distress." Disobedience and disloyalty bring defeat, loss of possession, inability—and (please note) divine hostility and opposition. There is such a thing as falling out of the power of God, a far more serious plight than falling into the power of Satan. Isaiah's vineyard was totally secure against marauders until disobedience came on the scene (Isa. 5:5).

In the ESV (Judg. 2:16) we read "Then," and of course, that is true enough, but the Hebrew simply says "and." In other words, there is something more to history than the rhythm of disobedience and defeat, although we must not forget that the Lord is not constrained by his own rhythms. He has a divine "And."

"Deliverance," says the hymn writer, "he affords to all who on his succour trust"[2]—true, but our passage says nothing about such trust. Deliverance comes simply and solely from the heart of God. This is why verse 17 goes on to underline the continuing backsliding of the people even when the judge-savior was raised up. They still "would not listen": they defected, proved disloyal, and turned from the commandments. So it was not their worthiness, their repentance, or anything else about them. It was sheer divine goodness and compassion (v. 18)—literally, "the Lord was moved to pity by their groaning." We will not leave verse 17 without noticing where the emphasis falls in the people's failings: the whole sad catalog falls within the brackets of "not listening" and "not walking in the commandments." The cardinal sin of the people of the Lord was always (and still is) to sit loose to the Word of God—in our terms, to possess the Scriptures but neglect them, to fail to prize, read, absorb, register, love, and obey. (See Amos 2:4; contrast Jer. 15:16.)

But there is, grimly, a limit to divine patience (Judg. 2:20–23). Here again, "So" (ESV) is reasonable as an interpretation, but (again) the Hebrew is simply "and"—a second and unwelcome "and," another way in which the Lord is unconstrained by his own rhythms. There comes a moment of turning away (Rom. 1:24, 26, 28). Yet, even so, positive purposes remain to be worked out. History is the arena of testing, for our good. The Lord longs for his people to walk in his way. The tests and trials of life (Judg. 2:22) are opportunities to demonstrate and prove devotion, loyalty, steadfastness. They are not meaningless or purposeless, nor are they accidental. The Lord says, "I will use them"—a gently paraphrased but acceptable rendering, and a real answer should the question "why?" arise to bother us. The Lord is at work and planning for our good, to bring us to a fresh point of commitment and consecration.

---

2. Nahum Tate and Nicholas Brady, "Through All the Changing Scenes of Life" (1696).

Day 5: An Occasional Blessing (2 Kings 22:1–20)

Old Testament history is not all doom and gloom! We can identify four major reforming kings, and you would get a central insight into Old Testament history if you found time to read about them: Asa, royal reform (1 Kings 15:9–24; 2 Chronicles 15–16); Uzziah/Azariah, priestly reform (2 Kings 15:1–6; 2 Chronicles 26); Hezekiah, prophetic reform (2 Kings 18–20; 2 Chronicles 29–32); and Josiah, law-book reform (2 Kings 22:1–23:30; 2 Chronicles 34–35). In a sense, though, they were interludes of light. They were all "flashes in the pan," and no lasting good was achieved. The inevitable end came with the capture and sacking of Jerusalem by the Babylonians in 586 BC, spelling the end of the visible monarchy of David, until the One came whose right it is to reign (Luke 1:32–33).

In some ways Josiah's reform is the most interesting as well as the most mysterious. What is this "Book of the Law" (2 Kings 22:8)? And how did it come to get lost? The favorite candidate is Deuteronomy (cf. Deut. 1:5; 4:44; 29:21; 30:10). But Exodus, Leviticus, and Numbers—or indeed the whole corpus of the books of Moses—could equally well be found to suit the details of Josiah's reform (cf. Ezra 3:2; 7:6, 10, 12, etc.). We do not know the answer to these questions; all we do know is that in Josiah's day a very covetable thing happened: the Word of God was rediscovered in the house of God and became the supreme authority in the kingdom. See what happened, and take note of the response. There is immediate recognition of the authority of the book as God's law (2 Kings 22:10–11), a dramatic reaction to its content (22:11), a determination to discover its true meaning (22:13–14), a national revival and commitment (23:1–3), a purging out of the false (23:4–7), and a reintroduction of forgotten divine ordinances of grace (23:21–23).

Unquestionably, this is the true way of reform: to rediscover the Word in the house of God, to set the Bible back at the head of church, nation, and individual life. If the voice of history speaks to today anywhere, it speaks here. But in Josiah's day it spoke too late; the issues were already settled beyond reform (23:26–27). Part of the essential definition of being human is our moral inheritance from the past. God is not mocked (Gal. 6:7), and he knows when, in mercy, to draw a line across the past and let holy judgment take its course (cf. Luke 11:47–51). The gross sins of Manasseh, Josiah's grandfather (2 Kings 21; 2 Chronicles 33), were too great a provocation. We have to recognize that "here we stand"—between the sins of the past, against whose malign consequences we pray for protection, and the challenge to rediscover for ourselves and to obey the Word of God.

Day 6: An Odd Way to Write History! (1 Kings 12:12–33)

Today's reading in 1 Kings 12 introduces us to the sad fact that David's kingdom was sundered in two. Following the mixed brilliance of Solomon, Rehoboam, by sheer pigheaded incompetence, failed to hold the kingdom together and watched the ten northern tribes—to be called Israel—separate under Jeroboam, leaving him with the tiny, two-tribe kingdom of Judah. So it remained until Israel succumbed to Assyria in 722 BC and Judah to Babylon in 586 BC. In Judah the line of David continued in unbroken succession; in Israel kings mounted the throne by their own abilities, very often through rebellion, for very few bequeathed the throne to their sons. The historian allows his spotlight to swing now north, now south, as he writes a sort of synoptic history of both kingdoms, and we need our wits about us to recall just where he is at any given moment. What an odd way to write history!

But there is a reason for it—a reason that reaches back to the book of Judges. The Judges historian noted the limited success of the "judges" (Judg. 2:6–18); he also noted the dark corruption of life at ground level (2:19). He reasoned that without a king, it had to be so (17:6; 18:1; 19:1; 21:25). In this way, the book of Judges starts what we may call the hunt for the true king. The first three kings all seemed to have messianic qualities, but Saul, David, and Solomon eventually revealed fundamental faults and failures. Following them, would the messianic king be found in the south, in the covenanted, orderly succession of the Davidic kings, father to son, for five centuries? Or could he be found in the naturally gifted, more charismatic aspirants to the northern throne, climbing to the top by their own ambitions and abilities? The answer was neither! King after king was labeled "disqualified." He was not like his father David (e.g., 1 Kings 15:3), or "he did what was evil in the sight of the LORD" (e.g., 15:26). Hope sprang eternal. Each successive king—in David's line—was crowned to the singing of Psalm 2, in the hope that he would prove to be the "son of God." But he never was, and that great hope extended into the undated future (e.g., Isa. 9:1), until a true and actual Son of God came to claim the throne.

The second book of Kings by its very structure summarizes the whole story. It starts with poor old David in the sad decline, physically and morally, of his dying days, a "toothless tiger" indeed, bequeathing to Solomon a last will and testament of which he should have been truly ashamed. Then comes the roll call of the failures, the long lines of kings who weren't up to the true mark of kingship. And finally, a tiny spark of hope. After thirty-seven years in Babylonian prison, "Jehoiachin king of Judah" emerges in the king's favor (2 Kings 25:27–30). David's sons will never actually reign again until Jesus comes, but David's line is not dead, and in that the Lord's promises to David live on and will be kept.

Four weeks of additional readings on Old Testament history are available in the appendix.

2

THE VOICE OF RELIGION

"Religion," says the *Chambers English Dictionary*, "is recognition of a higher, unseen, controlling power." Yes indeed, but there's more to it than that. Religion goes beyond merely "recognizing" a higher power; it is also responding to that power in acts and ceremonies. If the god is thought of in savage terms, then religion will take savage forms. So what about the Old Testament?

God Dwelling among His People

In Numbers 2 we are told how the camp of Israel was planned (see fig. 2.1). Actions speak louder than words. Could anything display more clearly that this God is one who chooses to live right at the heart of his people's life, and not only among them but also actually sharing their lot? For these were camping days; the people of God were on the march to Canaan from their slavery in Egypt, and to this tent-dwelling people the Lord said, "Make a tent for me and put it right at the center of your camp."

For the Lord's tent, we often use the traditional name "the tabernacle," but it was only a tent. They were tent dwellers, and their God chose to be a tent dweller with them, right at the heart of their life.

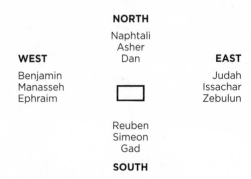

Figure 2.1   The arrangement of Israel's camp

Later, in the days of Solomon, the tent was replaced by a "house" (1 Kings 6:1), but the message was the same. The people now had houses, and once again, their God made his will known that he too would have a house and live among them. The house of the Lord in the Old Testament was not really like what we call a "church" (meaning a church building) today, even though we do refer to our church as "the house of God." Today, as his people, we "go to church" in order to be with him. In the Old Testament he came to his house in order to be among his people. He "indwelled" them by having his own house among their houses.

Haggai's Message

Now look at the message of the prophet Haggai. By his time the temple that Solomon had built was in ruins and had been so for seventy years since the Babylonians had demolished it in 586 BC, when the people went into exile in Babylon. But when Babylon fell in 539 BC to Cyrus the Persian, he allowed them to return (Ezra 1:1–3). After nineteen years back in their own land, however, this is what Haggai's perceptive prophetic eye saw (Hag. 1:6):

- The economy was in poor shape: "You have sown much, and harvested little."

- The people were dissatisfied: "You eat, but you never have enough; you drink, but you never have your fill. You clothe yourselves, but no one is warm."
- Inflation was rampant: "He who earns wages does so to put them into a bag with holes."

And what was the cause of this catalog of such modern-sounding ills? "This house lies in ruins" (v. 4).

It had been nearly twenty years since the exiles had been brought home from Babylon. In this time they had not done badly. They were living in paneled houses (v. 4), that is, stone houses with an inner lining of timber (the ancient equivalent of cavity-wall insulation). But the Lord's house was still unbuilt. It was still unrestored from the rubble of the Babylonian onslaught of almost a century earlier.

So was Haggai just concerned with bricks and mortar? Or was he simply a ritualist, offended because the full temple ceremonial was impossible while the temple was in ruins? It was neither of these things but rather that if people were not concerned to secure the living presence of the living God among them in the way that he had appointed, then they were opting for life without his presence (and blessing). They were choosing a go-it-alone lifestyle, a do-it-yourself society. If they didn't want him, they would have to do without what only he could supply.

What a message for Haggai's day—and ours. It does help us to see how seriously the Lord takes this matter of having a house among his people and living there. He comes not as an ornament or as a passive spectator but as the source of his people's well-being, prosperity, and fulfillment. Indeed, Haggai says that once they began to build the house, everything changed:

Consider from this day onward. . . . Since the day that the foundation of the LORD's temple was laid, consider. . . . [F]rom this day on I will bless you. (2:18–19)

The Lord God was once more dwelling among his people.

At Home but Not at Home

Yet it is not all smooth sailing to have God as one's neighbor. In the second half of the book of Exodus, the details of the "tabernacle" (the Lord's tent among his people's tents) are spelled out twice, first as a list of what was needed for the tent (chaps. 25–31) and then as a description of how the work was done (chaps. 35–40). Tremendous emphasis is laid on the fact of the Lord's dwelling among them, the preparation that must be made for his coming, and the detailed care taken to have everything just as he wanted it (cf. 25:9).

The Lord promised to come into his tent and meet his people: "There I will meet with the people of Israel. . . . I will dwell among the people of Israel and will be their God" (29:43, 45). This was the whole purpose of bringing them out of Egypt: "[I] brought them out of the land of Egypt that I might dwell among them" (v. 46).

Yet when all was finished and the tabernacle had been pitched for the first time, and when the Lord in his glory had indeed come into his tent, we read, "Moses was not able to enter the tent of meeting because the cloud settled on it, and the glory of the LORD filled the tabernacle" (40:35). If not even Moses could enter, then what price for the rest of us? The Lord was indeed at home among his people but not "at home" to callers!

The Lord's Cloud

In Exodus 3, Moses came face-to-face with the Lord for the first time. It is the famous incident of "the burning bush," as we call it, but in reality the bush did not burn at all:

> And the angel of the LORD appeared to him in [or "as"] a flame of fire out of the midst of a bush. He looked, and behold, the bush was burning, yet it was not consumed. (v. 2)

Here was an unusual thing—a flame that did not need fuel to feed it (as we saw earlier), a self-perpetuating flame. A *living* flame.

And as soon as Moses approached, the divine voice alerted him to two things: first, that the flame symbolized the divine presence; second, that in particular the flame stood for the holiness of God (vv. 2–5).

The story of the flame of fire continues at Mount Sinai: "Now Mount Sinai was wrapped in smoke because the LORD had descended on it in fire" (19:18). Commentators have been known to "explain" what happened at Sinai as volcanic action, but the Exodus account contradicts this, for here was not a fire that belched upward but a fire that came down: "The LORD came down on Mount Sinai, to the top of the mountain" (v. 20).

The message is the same as at the "burning bush": the holy God has come among his people. Hence the command, "Set limits around the mountain and consecrate it" (v. 23). To be sure, God was down among them, but once more his holiness kept them at a distance.

Always the "Sinai People"

As soon as the tabernacle was prepared, the stay at Sinai was over, but although they left the actual mountain behind, they carried the reality of Sinai with them: the holy God now lived among his people. The cloud on the tabernacle held at its heart the very fire of God (Ex. 40:35, 38). The tabernacle stood and was carried at the center of the people (Num. 2:17; 10:21).

God was with them and traveled with them, but he is the Holy One, and they must keep their distance. What does this holiness mean?

If we draw a diagram of the tabernacle from the details given in Exodus 25–31, it looks like the layout shown in figure 2.2. There was (1) the outer courtyard; (2) the "Holy Place," the first compartment of the tent itself; and (3) the "Most Holy Place" (26:31–33). In the Most Holy Place Moses was told to put, as its sole piece of furniture, the ark of the Lord, containing the stone tablets of the Ten Commandments (25:10–22). That was all. In pagan religions those who penetrated into the innermost sanctuary came face-to-face with some idol, but in the tabernacle they came face-to-face with the moral law.

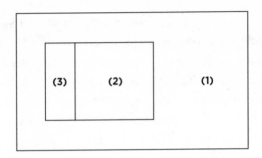

Figure 2.2   Tabernacle structure

This was the reason why no one could enter: no one was worthy. The holiness of the God of Israel is the moral holiness that the Ten Commandments express as his standard for our lives (Lev. 19:2). Until something is done to satisfy the demands of that law and to deal with the way we have broken it, the door into God's presence must remain shut in our faces.

The Holy God: Provider of Sacrifice

So "none could enter," but this is not the whole truth. The letter to the Hebrews summarizes the Old Testament exactly when it says, "But into the second [i.e., the Most Holy Place] only the high priest goes, and he but once a year, and not without taking blood" (Heb. 9:7).

The "ark," the box containing the Ten Commandments, had a very special lid (Ex. 25:17–22). It was called the "mercy seat" or "mercy cover" (v. 17 ESV mg.) and had to match the precise measurement of the ark itself (v. 17), providing an exact covering over the holy law that the ark contained.

The name "mercy cover" both describes what it did and explains what it was for. The Hebrew verb "to cover" means just that, as when Noah "covered" his ark (a different word for "ark" than that used for the one in the tabernacle) with pitch (Gen. 6:14). But in Old Testament religion the word developed a new, additional meaning. Sometimes when we hand over money to pay a bill, we say, "You'll find that that covers it": the payment "covers" the debt, not by hiding it out of sight (like pitch on the woodwork of the ark) but by canceling it out altogether.

This is how God provides "mercy," or atonement, for our sin: a price is paid that "covers" the debt, not sweeping it under the carpet but canceling it out by a full and equivalent payment.

Passover: The Blood of the Lamb

We can think about this important truth in two ways: first, through an event that illustrates atonement, and second, through a verse in which it is taught.

The event is the Passover. In Exodus 12 the situation is that the Lord plans to enter Egypt in judgment (v. 12), and the story answers the question of how we can be safe at such a time. Three words tell it all: the first is the word *satisfaction*. The Israelites were instructed that, in preparation for this night of divine judgment, they were to smear the blood of a sacrificed lamb around their doors (v. 7), relying on the Lord's promise that "the blood shall be a sign for you, on the houses where you are. And when I see the blood, I will pass over you" (v. 13). Not "when I see you," as if safety from divine judgment were an act of favoritism. No, there is something about the blood that turns the Lord from judgment to peace and satisfies him regarding the people in the blood-marked houses.

The second word is a counterpart of the first: *safety*. Since God is satisfied, the people are safe (v. 23), for, he promises, while the people remain where the blood was shed, there is no way that the destroyer can come in to hurt them.

But these two words demand an explanation: what is it about this blood that satisfies God and keeps his people safe? Verses 3 and 4 begin to point to the answer. The lamb chosen had to match exactly both the number of the people in each house and also their needs ("what each can eat"). There is, in this way, an exact equivalence between the animal that died and the people who take shelter under its blood.

But according to verse 30, "There was a great cry in Egypt, for there was not a house where someone was not dead." Divine judgment on those who had refused to obey God's Word took the token but dreadful form of the death in each Egyptian house of the firstborn son. In the houses of Israel the dead body was that of the carefully selected lamb. Our third word is, therefore, *substitution*. The death of a substitute "covered" Israel in the day of judgment, for, says Exodus 4:22, "Israel is my firstborn son."

The verse in which this lovely truth is taught is Leviticus 17:11. Speaking of the animal designated for sacrifice, it says,

> For the life of the flesh is in the blood, and I have given it for you on the altar to make atonement ["to pay the covering price"] for your souls, for it is the blood that makes atonement ["pays the covering price"] by ["as the equivalent to"] the life.

Look carefully at this verse. It teaches that one life is laid down as the equivalent of another, that this is the gift of God, and that the heart of the matter is the payment of the covering price. When the covering price is paid, the debt is discharged and gone forever.

The Day of Atonement

Once every year the high priest made atonement for the whole community (Leviticus 16). Two animals and two ceremonies were involved. One was hidden away within the tabernacle; the other was public, for all to see. Since the real problem of our sin is the broken law of God and the offense given to him as the Holy One, our first need is to bring the shed blood before him. So for the one and only time in the year, the high priest, carrying the blood of the sin offering (v. 15), went beyond the separating curtain into the Most Holy Place, and the "mercy cover," the exact covering of the law that had been broken, received the blood of a life laid down for the sins of the people.

All this was hidden away, however, and the Lord wanted his people to see, before their very eyes, the meaning and value of what had happened out of sight in his presence behind the curtain. So he ordered a second ceremony, in which the high priest laid his hands on the head of another beast and confessed over it all the people's sins (vv. 20–22). In this way he put their sins on the head of another. The animal became a sin bearer; the sins of the guilty passed to the account of the innocent. And as the people watched, the sin-bearing beast carried all their sins right away, never to be seen again.

At the Day of Atonement this was a communal exercise, but exactly the same thing happened individually and personally in every one of the sacrifices (e.g., 1:4; 3:2; 4:4, 24, 29). The Lord's provision was wonderful, simple, and merciful. The sinner identified the animal with his guilt and need before God, one died in the place of another, and atonement was made. This is the beating heart of Old Testament religion.

BIBLE READINGS
Old Testament Religion

Day 1: Exclusion and Inclusion (Ex. 40:33–Lev. 1:2)

To start with, we must understand more about the "tabernacle." We use this special word, but actually it is the ordinary word for a "tent." The Lord's people were a desert people, camping on their way to the Promised Land, and the Lord said, in effect, "If you're camping, I want to camp too" (cf. Ps. 34:7). The shape of the camp is found in Numbers 2. Think of the lines of Israel's tents going out in each direction in a cross-like formation, and right at the center, at the "crossing," they were to pitch the Lord's tent, where he would come and live at the very heart of his people (see fig. 2.1 on p. 38). This is the meaning of the tabernacle—the indwelling God. And according to Exodus 40:34, he did just that, in all his glory.

Everything, then, is now complete. See how Exodus 40 (vv. 16, 19, 21, 23, 25, 27, 29, 32) labors to assure us that all was in accordance with what the Lord wished. So he did actually come to live in the tent that he had commanded and that Moses "finished" (v. 33). Did Moses, then, think that he was free to come and go? Was he of the opinion that the indwelling God was "open to callers"? It was not to be so. The cloud was indeed a gracious provision for the guidance of the people in their travels (vv. 36–38), but it was also a symbol of the holiness of the great Indweller, and not even Moses was fit to enter that presence (v. 35). Yes, the Lord was with them, but no, they were not fit to be with him.

This is the point where we must read straight through from Exodus into Leviticus. Moses cannot enter, but then, out of the tabernacle a voice speaks, saying, literally, "When a person brings near a 'bring near' to Yahweh, from the herd, from the cattle, and from the flock, you must bring near your 'bring near'" (Lev. 1:2). With apologies for such a barbarous translation, please see the point: Moses cannot come near in his own person, yet there is a way to "come near" to the indwelling God—through the offerings and sacrifices with which the opening chapters of Leviticus are concerned. This is their point and purpose. The burnt offering (Leviticus 1) symbolized total commitment to the Lord (v. 13); the peace offering (chap. 3) spoke of rejoicing in the Lord's presence as though sitting down to a meal with him; the sin offering dealt with unfitness (chap. 4). In each case (1:4; 3:2; 4:4) the offerer lays his hand on the beast, appointing it to stand in his place (cf. 16:21–22) and bear his sin. The burnt offering and the sin offering thus "make atonement" (1:4; 4:20). The verb means "to cover." But in its religious use, it is the "covering price," the payment that "covers" and thereby cancels the debt. Through the death of the appointed beasts, our price is paid, and we may come near.

Day 2: Explaining the Unseen (Lev. 16:3–22)

The Day of Atonement was of major significance in the Old Testament calendar. It was the day when the people were granted clearance of every sin and made right with God. In yesterday's reading we noted that "atonement" meant the payment of the "covering price" that met and canceled every debt, and here we note how in Leviticus 16:21 all the main words of the vocabulary of sin are used, emphasizing the totality of the atonement provided: "sins" are the actual misdeeds of Israel, whether in thought, word, action, imagination, relationships with God or human beings—whatever. "Iniquities" translates a word meaning a "warp," a "twist," something deviant—the fatal inward defect in fallen human nature. And "transgressions" refers to rebellion, a willful refusal to obey, a deliberate choice of disloyalty. We cannot leave the blame with our fallen nature. (After all, a clock with a faulty spring can't be blamed for the wrong time.) No, we have deliberately chosen to oppose our God, to disobey, to rebel.

All this was dealt with in secret when the high priest sprinkled the blood on the "mercy cover," beneath which lay the tablets of the law of God (Ex. 40:20), the law that we broke in our rebellion and that constitutes our condemnation. The blood has paid the price for us (see the reading for day 3 below): all is covered (see Lev. 16:30).

But this was done out of sight. No one entered with the high priest (v. 17), and even he was obliged to shroud the whole exercise in a cloud of incense for his own protection (v. 13; contrast Heb. 9:24: Jesus alone can "appear" before God). The importance of the visible ceremony of the scapegoat (Lev. 16:10) is that the people may actually see portrayed before their eyes the central significance of what happened in secret; they can watch their sins being borne by another and carried away to be seen no more. The laying on of hands (v. 21) is plainly the appointment of a substitute—this one, this "innocent," "perfect" beast, will stand in the place of the sinner who otherwise would bear his own sin. And as the hands are held in place, every transgression is recited, so that (so to speak) the high priest's arms become a sort of "moral bridge" over which Israel's sins are conveyed to rest on the other who becomes a sin bearer (v. 22).

All this is, of course, a preview of Jesus and the cross. Hebrews 10 brings the truth to its final form: first, by reminding us that "the blood of bulls and goats" cannot "take away sins" (v. 4), and second, by telling us why Jesus can—because he alone brings not only his sinless body and person to the sacrifice but also (which the beast could never do) his consenting will to stand in our place (v. 7), so that the act of substitution is at last complete. Jesus has offered "for all time a single sacrifice for sins" (v. 12).

Day 3: One Key Verse (Lev. 17:11)

This may very well be the only verse in the Old Testament that actually goes into a detailed explanation of the meaning and reason why the sacrifices "work." The ESV fixes one meaning on the wording, but in fact it is much richer.

1. When Leviticus 17:11 says "the life . . . is in the blood," the meaning is that blood is the principle of life in humans and animals. Blood conjoined with flesh constitutes a living being. Blood in separation from flesh indicates that death has taken place. Compare this verse with Genesis 9:4–6, where "shedding blood" describes a violent death. So it is throughout the Bible, in our present usage, in common sense, and especially in the sacrifices: the "blood" points to a life taken. For example, in Exodus 12:6, 7, 13, the evidence of "blood" meant that the Passover Lamb had been slaughtered and was lying dead (and roasted) in the houses of Israel.

2. "I have given it for you" (Lev. 17:11) states a fundamental principle of biblical religion. The sacrifices are not a human device to put pressure on the holy God—that is the way every other religion operates, the principle of meritorious "works," of human acts to win/compel divine favor. Here it is the Lord providing a solution to the dilemma of human sin and unworthiness, the religion of divine action, of grace.

3. "Atonement" (Lev. 17:11), as ever, speaks in religion of the "covering price." Genesis 6:14 exemplifies the secular use of the verb in its meaning "to cover," but in its religious usage it always has a "price-paying" significance—the payment that "covers" (and thereby cancels) the debt.

4. Many books on the Old Testament advocate the strange view that "blood" signifies "life released from its nexus with the flesh" and therefore is available as a "gift of life" to present to the offended God. This "gift" is then assumed (somehow) to satisfy him or to constitute a "shield" between him and the sinner. In any case, it gives us a chance to "do something" of a protective, prophylactic, remedial nature in relation to our need, but of course, it is, first, an offense to common sense. Whoever looked on violently shed blood and immediately thought of life released, life in independence from flesh? Second, it subverts the whole ethos of biblical religion: the religion of grace and divine provision becomes the religion of endeavor and human action. But the words "on the altar" (Lev. 17:11) restore a true perspective. The "altar" is the place of death—indeed, the consigning of the already dead animal to the flames of divine holy wrath.

5. Literally, Leviticus 17:11 reads, "to make atonement for your souls [i.e., 'to place a covering over your souls'], for the blood it is that pays the covering price taking the place of / at the expense of the soul." Either translation is possible; both should be held together. The first refers to the "soul" of the sinner, who needs the mercy cover: that "soul/life" would itself pay the price of its own sin had God not provided the sacrifice as his remedy for

sin (Gen. 22:7–8). The second rendering refers to the "soul/life" of the slaughtered beast, the life laid down in payment.

The sacrifices were essentially substitutionary, price-paying, and expressive of the principle that "the wages of sin is death" (Rom. 6:23).

Day 4: Not Ritual but Repentance (Pss. 50:5–23; 51:1–3)

"Religion" inevitably comes to involve the repetitive (for who can be endlessly inventive?) and therefore the familiar, and the familiar can so easily become the automatic. So we can go through the motions, conform to the accepted, and acquiesce in a religion devoid of moral and spiritual growth, a religion that (so to speak) "walks with people" (reproducing the "norm") but no longer "walks with God." This is what Jeremiah had in mind when he spoke of treating the temple as "a den of robbers" (Jer. 7:11)—a place of security to which they retire and from which they emerge exactly the same robbers who went in. It is at the heart of Psalm 50. In verses 8–13 the accusation is of thinking of religious observance as "doing God a good turn"; in verses 16–21 it is religion without moral and spiritual values. The former speaks of human arrogance and insults the living God; the latter speaks of human flippancy and insults the holy God. Both are still distinctly possible and evident avenues of declension and corruption of the ideal and are exemplified today.

Together Psalms 50–51 offer antidotes, each in its own context. Psalm 50:14a and 23a call, first, for the thankful heart. Thanksgiving not only recognizes the constant goodness of the Lord but also imparts a living sense of his nearness, his sensitivity to our needs, his unmerited favors, all we owe to him each and every day. Thanksgiving, therefore, counters sameness, familiarity, the staleness that can infect the religious round. Psalm 50 goes on to add, secondly, the living reality of a consecrated response to divine goodness (v. 14b); thirdly, the vivacity imparted to "religion" by prayer as the way to deal with the actualities of life, and the joyful invigoration imparted by answered prayer (v. 15); and fourthly, a life focused (not on "religious activity" but) on the central wonder of our salvation (v. 23b).

Psalm 51 adds, fifthly, the simple and effective way of repentance to deal with all our sin. Look at the nine great terms in verses 1–2: three point to what God is ("mercy," "love," "abundant mercy" [or "compassion," NIV]), three to what is desired of him ("blot out," "wash," "cleanse"), and three to our need ("transgressions," "iniquity," "sin"). The single, all-embracing remedy that will bring us into this storehouse of benefit is captured in this phrase: "for/because I know/acknowledge my transgressions, and my sin is ever before me" (v. 3). To live (as someone has said) keeping short accounts with God: the life of repentance.

Day 5: The Call to Obey (Isa. 1:10–20)

"The more the merrier" seems to be the preferred motto of religion. The Lord commanded the offerings he desired, usually single beasts; religion went in for "a multitude," to give God more than "enough" (Isa. 1:11). Amos saw the same error—annual sacrifices "every morning," the triennial tithe "every three days"—and he put his finger on the problem: "so you love to do"—the divine will subjected to the human cult of "helpfulness" and self-pleasing (Amos 4:4–5). Isaiah put it down to a faulty theology, as if God were himself "religious" and subject to "the more the merrier" thinking.

He also saw formalism—a mere "trampling of my courts" (Isa. 1:12); acquiring a certificate of good behavior for sheer attendance; a religion of the act without the heart (lit., "offerings of falsehood," v. 13); hypocritical, outward pretense; and (maybe above all) a dire mixture of religious punctiliousness and personal wrongdoing. To paraphrase verse 13b, "I cannot be doing with religious exactitude alongside moral deviancy." The latter infects even great exercises like prayer, where we might think that at last we were out of the arena of "religion" and into the more congenial arena of personal devotion. But look at the uplifted hands in verse 15b, which literally reads, "Your hands? With violently shed blood they are full!" True religion needs the heart engaged; true religion demands a conformed, matching life; true religion is more than marking an attendance card. It is commitment, concern, moral and spiritual involvement; it looks for the purity of holiness. It all stands to reason, what is the point of a burnt offering without making our total self-offering, or a fellowship offering without a desire for the Lord's goodwill and companionship, or a sin offering without repentance and works worthy of repentance (Luke 3:8)?

Consequently, Isaiah calls first for a proper use of the means of grace (Isa. 1:14a), the washing and cleansing for which the Lord provided his ordinances of washing and blood shedding; then for serious reformation, of conduct (v. 16b) and mind (v. 17a); next for social redress on behalf of "justice" (better, "judgment," i.e., making the right decisions at the right time) and against oppressors (v. 17b); and finally for identification with those at the bottom of society's heap (v. 17c). James had many of the same ideas (James 1:26–27).

How very practical, down-to-earth, and specific Old Testament religion is. And behind it all, the glorious reality of the Lord, offering cleansing, ready to exchange the scarlet of our guilt for his snowy purity (Isa. 1:18; Rev. 1:14), ever reminding us and calling us to the foundational principle behind all Old Testament thinking: to obey what "the mouth of the LORD has spoken" (Isa. 1:20).

Day 6: The Heart of True Religion
(Jer. 31:31–34; Mic. 6:6–8; 7:18–20)

Worship, I have heard it said, is actually "worth-ship." Is this true? At any rate it points us helpfully in the right direction. Worship is recognition of the *worth* of God, according him that *worth*, and responding to his *worthiness* in wonder, love, and praise. Some translations, in their literal way, invite us to "bless the Lord" (e.g., Ps. 103:1 ESV, NKJV). When we ask him to bless us or some friend, we know that we are using a shorthand for "Please, Lord, review my situation, identify my needs, and respond by meeting them." So when we bless the Lord, we review not his needs but his perfections, and we respond by giving him the worship that is his due.

Jeremiah 31:31–34 reveals the God of the new covenant. The word "covenant" first appears in the Bible in Genesis 6:18. Its background is a divine work of grace: "Noah found favor" (v. 8)—the sheer, unmerited, undeserved grace of God, who set Noah apart for salvation in a world under just condemnation (which, left to himself, Noah shared). The covenant expressed that salvation as a solemn divine promise and undertaking. Now Jeremiah takes the matter forward to its ultimate perfection: Moses bequeathed his covenant on stone tablets; the "new covenant" (Jer. 31:31) is written on the heart. That is, it rests, first, on a divine work of regeneration, the renewal of human nature into a shape designed for obeying and matching God's law, and second, on God's promise (which Jeremiah does not explain, but we know the explanation), "I will forgive their iniquity, and I will remember their sin no more" (v. 34)—such a divine dealing with and settlement of our sins that they no longer exist even as a divine memory.

Micah 6 takes the next step. What the Lord looks for is not "religion"—no, not even in the most extreme expressions of religious devotion (vv. 6–7)—but literally, "judgment . . . loyal, committed love and devotion . . . humility" (v. 8). "Judgment" is one of the Old Testament words for judicial, authoritative decisions made by the Lord (e.g., Deut. 5:1 [ESV: "rules"]), which are therefore revelations of his mind and will—not condemnatory but decisive, settling issues, putting things to rights, letting us know what is his will. In the Hebrew the vocabulary of "love" (ESV: "kindness") in Micah represents love affirmed as a decision of the will (other words express love as a heart emotion). This word is the love affirmed in a wedding service; it is "till death do us part"—and beyond—love. It is the ever-unchanging, devoted love of the Lord for his own, and it is the way we are called to love him back, and then to love each other. "To walk humbly" corresponds to the great New Testament word "humble-mindedness" (e.g., "humbleness of mind," Col. 3:12 KJV). The Old Testament rendering catches it exactly.

Finally, Micah 7 sets the seal on the whole issue of the Lord and our sin. What a picture! What a reality! Pardon, forgiveness, anger that has passed, steadfast (unchanging, committed) love, every iniquity "cast" into the depths of the sea (v. 19). How we should accord worth-ship to such a worthy God.

Four weeks of additional readings on Old Testament religion are available in the appendix.

3

THE VOICE OF WORSHIP

A Window

The Psalms are our window into the Old Testament. We look through them, and we actually see what it was like to be a believer in those old covenant times. What surprise and delight await us! Indeed, the men and women of the Old Testament often put us to shame by the reality, the personal quality, the joy, the exuberance, and the knowledge of God that are so clear in their worship and song.

Knowing God

Look how well they knew God. Here are some verses from Psalm 18. Read them slowly. Think about each word:

> I love you, O LORD, my strength.
> The LORD is my rock and my fortress and my deliverer,
> my God, my rock, in whom I take refuge,
> my shield, and the horn of my salvation, my
> stronghold.
> I call upon the LORD, who is worthy to be praised.
> (vv. 1–3)

Corresponding to this deep knowledge of who and what God is, there is a matching spirit of devotion captured well in Psalm 119:

> I have chosen the way of faithfulness;
>> I set your rules before me.
> I cling to your testimonies, O LORD. (vv. 30–31)

> Oh how I love your law!
>> It is my meditation all the day. (v. 97)

> How sweet are your words to my taste,
>> sweeter than honey to my mouth! (v. 103)

Or again, God was at the center of their approach to life, even in its severest testings. Psalm 74 is typical in two ways: first, it faces up to the real awfulness of life. It does not pretend that things are other or better than they are. But then, in the teeth of that awfulness, it asserts what is true about God:

> Direct your steps to the perpetual ruins;
>> the enemy has destroyed everything in the sanctuary! (v. 3)

> Yet God my King is from of old,
>> working salvation in the midst of the earth. (v. 12)

School atlases used to go out of their way to make sure that we knew the comparative size of each country. If England and Australia can both fill the same-sized page, how were children to know that the one was so immensely bigger than the other? Well, in the corner of the Australia page there would be a tiny, postage-stamp-sized England, with the words, "England on the same scale."

The Psalms do the same thing but in reverse. Alongside the problems of life, they set a huge reality: "God on the same scale." This is what Psalm 74 is doing. Although its problems look like "perpetual ruins" that all the time in the world could not mend, the great King is still on his throne.

This approach to things is constant in the Psalms. Amid an endless variety of earthly crises and challenges to faith—national, personal, social, and domestic, with problems of inequality, suffering, injustice, depression, and disappointment—each map of trouble is accompanied by another that reduces it to its proper proportions: the greatness of the Lord in position, power, and salvation.

Prayer, Forgiveness, Hope, and Joy

Along with this grasp of the greatness of God goes a vigorous confidence in prayer:

> Give ear, O LORD, to my prayer;
> > listen to my plea for grace.
> In the day of my trouble I call upon you,
> > for you answer me. (Ps. 86:6–7)

And there is so much more, but we must be content for the moment with three further aspects of the Psalms. First, the psalmists knew what it meant to be right with God. What about this, regarding the forgiveness of sins?

> If you, O LORD, should mark iniquities,
> > O Lord, who could stand?
> But with you there is forgiveness. . . .
>
> > For with the LORD there is steadfast love,
> > and with him is plentiful redemption. (130:3–4, 7)

Furthermore, the Psalms were not afraid to say "afterward," pointing to the life to come:

> Nevertheless, I am continually with you;
> > you hold my right hand.
> You guide me with your counsel,
> > and afterward you will receive me to glory. . . .
> My flesh and my heart may fail,
> > but God is the strength of my heart and my portion
> > > forever. (73:23–24, 26)

And finally, what exuberance they enjoyed in worship!

> Clap your hands, all peoples!
>   Shout to God with loud songs of joy! (47:1)

> God has gone up with a shout,
>   the LORD with the sound of a trumpet. (v. 5)

> Praise him with tambourine and dance;
>   praise him with strings and pipe!
> Praise him with sounding cymbals;
>   praise him with loud clashing cymbals!
> Let everything that has breath praise the LORD!
> Praise the LORD! (150:4–6)

The Content and Origin of the Psalms

So often we look into the Old Testament through the window of the Pharisees as we meet them in the New Testament: joyless people, carping, critical, laden with the dust of man-made tradition, their lives cramped and distorted by human regulations (Matt. 15:3, 6–9). We need to remember that the Lord Jesus spoke of the Pharisees as "a plant his heavenly Father did not plant" (Matt. 15:13). This means that far from being typical Old Testament people, the Pharisees were, in relation to the Old Testament, what we would call "heretics" and not "Exhibit A" of the Old Testament church at all.

No, it is in the Psalms that we see firsthand the real Old Testament religion and worship with all its joyousness, its delight and spiritual confidence, its true knowledge of God, and its simplicity of trust in him for time and eternity.

The passages already quoted show the way in which the Psalms arose from actual experiences of life in both joy and sorrow. One person's experiences, David's, loom very large, but he was by no means the only one. Here are some examples:

- Experiences of life: joys (Psalms 92; 113), sorrows (Psalms 42; 88)

- David's experiences: personal (Psalms 3; 18; 34), royal (Psalms 101; 110)
- Religious experiences: processions (Psalms 24; 118), "pilgrim praise" (Psalms 120–134)

All this abundance of poetry and song is spread over nearly a thousand years. Psalm 90 is attributed to Moses, and very likely the title covers Psalm 91 as well. At the other end of the period stands Psalm 137, which looks back, possibly from a fairly close vantage point, to the experience of exile in Babylon.

Insofar as it is possible to date the bulk of the Psalms within the history of Israel, it might look something like figure 3.1.

1000 BC	586 BC	520 BC
David/Solomon . . . reforming kings First temple . . . temple recovery . . . pilgrim feasts	Exile	Return Second temple
The psalms of David Pilgrim psalms (120–134; etc.) Kingship praise (93–100) Praise collections (113–118; 146–150) Choir repertoires (42–49; 72–83) The choirmaster collection (51–62; etc.)		Formation of the book of Psalms

Figure 3.1   Dating of the Psalms

This diagram oversimplifies very complicated questions, and there is so much we just do not know. How were individual psalms preserved? How were they edited into groups and small collections, what we would call "hymnbooks"? Who was "the choirmaster," who is mentioned fifty-five times (e.g., Psalms 4; 5; 6), and what did he do? Why are the psalms of David scattered as they are? And why do the small "hymnbooks" (e.g., Psalms 93–100; 120–134) appear where they do in the final Psalter?

On the other hand, in spite of all this ignorance, there is no reason to doubt that the vast majority of the psalms were written before the exile or that the ascription, literally, "To David" was intended to signify David's authorship.

The First (i.e., Solomon's) Temple

The period of the monarchy saw great "reformations" of religion under Asa (1 Kings 15:11–15), Jehoshaphat (1 Kings 22:41–46; 2 Chron. 17:7–9; 19:4–11), Joash (2 Kings 11–12; 2 Chronicles 24), Hezekiah (2 Kings 18:1–4; 2 Chronicles 29–31), and Josiah (2 Kings 22–23; 2 Chronicles 34–35). These reforms refocused national life on the temple, and it is sensible to think that they would have stimulated the collection of inherited worship songs for use in the reformed temple. Certainly, the headings and the text of the Psalms suggest how they were used in worship. Psalm 45 and many others indicate the tune to be used; the word "song" in the heading to Psalm 48 and elsewhere indicates musical accompaniment; the little word "selah," which is sprinkled throughout the Psalms (e.g., 46:3, 7, 11), has so far defied explanation both as a word and as to its use, but it was probably some sort of divider, maybe indicating a pause for meditation when the psalm was sung in worship.

The Second (i.e., Postexilic) Temple

By the time the second temple was built (Ezra 3; 6:13–22; Haggai 1–2) in 520–516 BC, there was a rich harvest of songs waiting to be gathered into a larger hymnbook, and we can attribute the production of the Psalter as we know it to the religious leaders of that time.

Worship

What is this worship of which the Psalms are the vocal expression? An easy way to get a taste (but no more than a taste) of worship in the Old Testament is through the key words that show us worship in action. From these we learn something very important indeed. Old Testament religion was often outwardly complicated, involving all the rituals of the book of Leviticus. Also, it was often very exuberant and noisy. But at its center there was a still, even solemn, heart of devotion, a wondering awareness of God, and the realization that before such an awesome God only the lowest place befits his worshipers.

Psalm 95:6 gathers three such verbs together: "Oh come, let us *worship* and *bow down*; let us *kneel* before the LORD, our Maker!" It is not important to try to make distinctions between the three verbs but rather to feel their cumulative force as worshipers bring themselves down ("worship") and down lower ("bow down") and then lower still ("kneel").

Such was the reaction of Elijah before the awesomeness of "the God who answers by fire" when he, literally, "crouched on the ground" in acknowledgment and in submissive waiting for God (1 Kings 18:24, 38, 42).

In Psalm 95, however, it was not, as for Elijah, fire from heaven that prompted this self-humbling worship but the works of God in salvation and providential care. He is our "Maker" (v. 6), in the sense that by his choice, out of all who live on earth, he "made" us his people. Having chosen to do so, he has never ceased to tend us as our Shepherd-God, leading us from pasture to pasture, keeping us as "the sheep of his hand" (v. 7). In this way worship is a response to revealed truth: the truth of God our Savior.

Responding: The Lord's Name

Psalm 104:35–105:3 offers us a whole cluster of verbs of vocal response: "Bless the LORD, O my soul"; "praise the LORD"; "give thanks to the LORD"; "call upon his name"; "sing to him"; make music ("sing praises," ESV) to him; "tell of all his wondrous works"; "glory in his holy name."

Notice that twice in these verses the "name" of the Lord is praised. His "name" is shorthand for all that he has revealed himself to be. In other words, worship arises out of what the Lord has said about himself. It is governed neither by human tradition (cf. Mark 7:5–7) nor by what we may from time to time find helpful (cf. Amos 4:4–5) but only by the revelation of his name and what he has done (his "wonders" performed in the salvation of his people).

Blessing the Lord

Meditating on these truths leads us to praise God for himself and for his works and to give thanks for the heavenly benefits he has given us. The lovely expression "to bless the Lord" has sadly disappeared from some modern translations, and yet it seems to have a very special meaning. When the Lord "blesses" us (the same word is used), he reviews what we are—in unworthiness, need, difficulty, and so on—and responds in mercy and grace, timely help, strength, and provision. When we bless the Lord (as we touched on earlier), we review what he is—in his heavenly and eternal glory, in his revealed attributes, in the love and grace of his salvation, in his daily works of providence and care—and we respond point by point, in wonder, love, and praise. This is worship.

Songs That Must Remain Unsung?

But can we use all the psalms? The vast majority, of course, delight us, and those of us who grew up singing the Psalms as a regular part of Sunday worship found no difficulty in adding as a concluding refrain, "Glory be to the Father and to the Son and to the Holy Spirit," for the sentiments we expressed in song matched the New Testament revelation of God in Christ.

But what about the following?

> Oh that you would slay the wicked, O God! . . .
> Do I not hate those who hate you, O LORD? . . .
> I hate them with complete hatred;
>   I count them my enemies. (Ps. 139:19–22)

Or,

> Let death steal over them;
>   let them go down to Sheol alive. (55:15)

About twenty-four psalms contain passages like these and make us wonder why they are in the Bible at all, in what sense they can be "the Word of God," and if we should be expected to use them.

Many commentators take an easy way out. They describe these "offending" passages as "Old Testament morality," which has now been left behind by the superior revelation of God in Christ. But this will not do, for in the New Testament—indeed, on the lips of Jesus—we find, "Woe to you, scribes and Pharisees, hypocrites! . . . You serpents, you brood of vipers, how are you to escape being sentenced to hell?" (Matt. 23:29, 33). And we find Paul saying, "If anybody is preaching to you a gospel contrary to the one you received, let him be accursed!" (Gal. 1:9). There is also the cry of the saints in heaven, "O Sovereign Lord, holy and true, how long before you will judge and avenge our blood on those who dwell on the earth?" (Rev. 6:10).

The point must be made that indignation expressed in forceful terms is not confined to the Old Testament. It is an aspect of the whole Bible and of the Lord Jesus himself. But we must take care to note that, with respect to the Old Testament as much as the New, vengefulness in thought or deed is expressly forbidden:

> You shall not hate your brother in your heart. . . . You shall not take vengeance or bear a grudge. (Lev. 19:17, 18)

> Do not say, "I will repay evil";
>   wait for the LORD, and he will deliver you. (Prov. 20:22)

Romans 12:19 and Deuteronomy 32:35 bind the two Testaments together on this topic.

We begin to see some daylight regarding the verses that at first sight offend us when we notice that they are all prayers. We misread them if we see them as evidence of a vengeful spirit, or if we understand them as setting out a program for human action. On the contrary, they are an exercise of committing the problem to the Lord and leaving it there. Far from backing away from these verses in the Psalms, we, who belong to an age that hastens to take vengeance and to solve its problems with bombs, should rather admire and desire the spirit that flew to prayer and left it at that.

There remains, of course, the vigorous way in which the prayers were phrased. Here is an example that startles us by its plain speaking and at the same time illustrates why the psalmists felt that they could pray as they did:

> Appoint a wicked man against him;
>> let an accuser stand at his right hand.
> When he is tried, let him come forth guilty. (Ps. 109:6–7)

In this psalm David is enduring false, malicious accusation. Now according to God's law in Deuteronomy 19:16–19, the punishment of a false witness is to suffer what he would have inflicted. Possibly, were we placed in a Psalm 109 situation, we would cry out, "Lord, please deal with this trouble!" and leave it at that. But because God is unchanging, he will answer that prayer by bringing on the accusers what they would have done to us. That is his way.

In other words, where we would pray *blandly*, the Psalms pray *realistically*, facing up to the implications of what they are asking.

We need to stop backing off from these bits of the psalms that, initially, are difficult to take. Most of them arise, like Psalm 109, from Deuteronomy 19:16–19. God's legal principle expressed there is that the wrongful accuser will receive what he wrongly planned to inflict. That is what God is like. That is the way he runs his world.

Our problem is put in a nutshell by Psalm 143:11–12. We would find no difficulty in praying verse 11: "For your name's sake, O LORD, preserve my life." But what about verse 12? "In your unfailing love, silence [i.e., in death] my enemies" (NIV).

Surely it is worth wondering if our unease arises from an absence of *holy* anger and *righteous* moral outrage in our makeup? The fact that we may possibly be unable to pray such prayers without a sinful, vengeful spirit creeping in is not to say that no one can.

Certainly, it is much, much nearer the truth to say that the psalmists who could and did pray in this way were ahead of us in holiness than to dismiss their prayers as evidence of a lower morality.

Do the Psalms Point to the Lord Jesus Christ?

From a very early point in Old Testament times there was a longing for a king. This is reflected in Judges 17:6: "In those days there was no king in Israel. Everyone did what was right in his own eyes" (cf. 18:1).

The assumption behind these verses is that "if only we had a king, all this religious heresy [Judges 17], social unrest [Judges 18], and moral corruption [Judges 19–21] would be dealt with: things would be just perfect." But of course, when they did get a king, they found that they had to rephrase their hopes. They had to begin to say, "If only we had a *perfect* king . . . !"

But such a person was not to be found. In the books of Kings the spotlight swings to and fro from the ordered succession of Davidic kings in the south to the quickly changing kings of the north. But they were all alike, failures personally and politically, and the perfect king bringing the perfect society remained an unfulfilled hope.

But hope sprang out of disappointment and developed in intensity. The Psalms reflect it as they sing of a king who faces world opposition (2:1–3; 110:1–2) but is victorious (45:3–5; 89:22–23). By the Lord's help (18:46–50; 21:1–13) he establishes world rule (2:8–12; 45:17; 72:8–11; 110:5–6), which is based at Zion (2:6) and marked by righteousness (45:4, 6–7; 72:2–3; 101:1–8). His rule is everlasting (21:4; 45:6; 72:5), peaceful (72:7), prosperous (72:16), and devoted (72:5). The king is preeminent among people (45:2, 7), friend of the poor, and enemy of the oppressor (72:2–4, 12–14). He owns an everlasting name (72:17) and enjoys everlasting blessing (45:2). He is heir to David's covenant (89:28–37; 132:11–12) and to Melchizedek's priesthood (110:4). He belongs to the Lord (89:18), is his Son (2:7; 89:27), sits at his right hand (110:1), and is himself divine (45:6).

It is very likely that these psalms were used as coronation anthems, sung before the new king as he took his throne, in order to "hold him to the highest." But the reality was always more than any mere son of David could be. It awaited the unique Son of David who is also the Son of God (Luke 1:32).

A Main Lesson: Take It to the Lord

Psalms is the longest book in the Bible. It is gloriously varied in style, subjects, thoughts, poetic expression, and literary form. Surely it is a bit ambitious to ask if there is one line of thought that runs through it all. If anything can make a bid to be such a single line of thought, it is this: take it to the Lord in prayer.

In the Psalms we meet people in sickness (88:15), persecution (143:11–12), loneliness (142:4), joy (145:1, 21), and so on. But they have this in common: that they are determined to bring all of life to the Lord in committed, urgent prayer. Surrounded by troubles, they stop to remember him, how great he is, the wonders he has done (74:12–17; 77:7–12; 78:9–11). They know how meaningful and essential it is to give up listening to themselves and their troubles and to start talking to themselves about a great, sovereign, loving, and unforgetting God. He is a God who will prove to be sufficient as they lean on him in the present (23:1–6; 121:1–8) and whose promises guarantee a future where all will be well (96:11–13).

BIBLE READINGS
Old Testament Worship

Day 1: Worship in Line with the Word (Gen. 4:1–15)

In day 6 of the readings on Old Testament religion (p. 52), we saw a link between religion and worship; in today's reading from

Genesis 4 we learn again the basic issue involved. The story of Cain and Abel is one of the many places where we really wish the Bible gave us more information. We can only read between the lines and hope to reach the truth.

1. What does Eve's outcry at the birth of Cain mean? Was it a word of humility? "I have gotten a man with the help of the LORD" (Gen. 4:1). Or was it a word of arrogance: "Along with Yahweh [i.e., 'like Yahweh'] I have created . . ." (cf. 14:19 ESV mg. for the meaning "create" for this verb)? If the latter, then from birth Cain was set on the way of pride, which was later his downfall. But possibly we are meant to leave the words as ambiguous, in which case Cain is faced with a choice: humility or pride.

2. Yahweh's word to Cain in verses 6–7 indicates that (somehow) Cain knew the difference between what was right and what was not right in the matter of his and his brother's gift. He was also aware that sin was involved and that it was "crouching" at his door like a beast at rest, either to rise and overpower him or to be overpowered by him. Where did such knowledge come from?

3. We have to assume at this point that Yahweh had already made his desires known—that true worship meant blood sacrifice. Could it have been when the Lord God made garments of skins (3:21) that he explained the significance of sacrifices, blood, and death?

4. We ought to notice that Abel made his offering after careful consideration—"firstborn . . . fat portions" (4:4)—whereas Cain (it seems) just brought whatever was at hand, "some of the fruits" (4:3 NIV). In a word, the disposition of the offerer is important.

If we are at all moving along the right lines (and at least it all concurs with what we learn throughout the Bible), then as a basic rule, worship must rest on, and be obedient to, a previously revealed will of God. We are not free to be self-pleasing. Worship is not an area in which personal choice and what we might find "helpful" are in order. As Calvin remarks on Matthew 15:9, "True religion must be conformable to the will of God as its unerring standard."[1] Jesus was, if anything, sharper: worship that is no more than a human device is "vain" (Matt. 15:9). This was the pit into which Cain fell, where arrogance, pride, and sinful animosity bound him and turned him into a brother-hating murderer (1 John 3:11–15). And indeed, we need to keep our traditions of worship constantly under review, with ceaseless reformation and adjustment according to the Word of God, lest our coming together be condemnation rather than blessing.

Day 2: Worship in the "Name" of the Lord (Gen. 12:8–13:4; Ex. 3:13–15)

I want to take only two verses from this rather discreditable incident in the story of Abraham (Gen. 12:8–13:4): the first and the last. We know few, if any, details about how the patriarchs worshiped, but these verses reveal a worship centered on the Lord's name and involving sacrifice. As to the latter, 22:13 uses the key words "instead of" and shows that they understood the principle of a substitutionary death. As to the name of the Lord, things are both more complex and richer.

From the earliest days (4:26) the "name" Yahweh was known and used in worship, but Genesis contains no indication of any particular significance or meaning attached to that name. It was simply the name of their God. If questioned as to his nature, they would have replied, as in Genesis 17:1, "The LORD appeared to Abram and said to him, 'I am God Almighty [*El Shaddai*].'" The patriarchs had a rich theology based on the noun *El*, meaning "God in transcendent majesty and power": *El Elyon*, "God Most High" (14:22); *El Bethel*, "God of Bethel" (31:13); *El Roi*, "God of seeing" (16:13); *El Elohe Israel*, the transcendent One who is "the God of Israel" (33:20 ESV mg.); *El Olam*, "the Everlasting God" (21:33). Above all, there was *El Shaddai* (17:1; 28:3; 35:11; 43:14; 48:3).

---

1. John Calvin, *Institutes of the Christian Religion*, trans. Henry Beveridge, 1559 ed. (Edinburgh: London, 1863), 1.4.3.

It remains uncertain what *Shaddai* means. "Almighty" (ESV) serves well and gives the right idea, but examination of the contexts in which the title occurs suggests a closer definition: *El Shaddai* is the God who is at his most powerful when human strength and resources are at their lowest ebb. Just the God, for example, when Jacob, the lonely, homeless traveler, was heading into the unknown and about to spend his first night under the stars (28:3).

It was Moses's privilege to become the bearer of the meaning of the name Yahweh (the only "name" among all the nouns). In reply to the question "What are you?" Yahweh would have replied, "I am God Almighty"; in reply to the question "Who are you?" he would have said, "I am Yahweh," his personal name, which Exodus 3:14 defines by the enigmatic "I AM WHO I AM." This means that only he knows who he is and that we must wait for him, if he so will, to reveal himself. He did so to Moses: first in words, forecasting his coming actions and their meaning, and then in confirmatory action at the exodus (Exodus 3–15), so that, in brief, Yahweh is the God who saves his people and overthrows their enemies; he is the God of liberation and redemption (6:6), the God who vows to take and keep a people for himself (6:7), and who honors his promises to the letter (Josh. 21:43–45).

To worship him is to "bless his name" (Ps. 96:2): to review the excellencies he has revealed—in titles and in the name—about himself, and to respond in wonder, love, and praise, indeed, in adoration.

Day 3: The Tent of Meeting (Ex. 33:7–11)

The tabernacle, the Lord's tent, was, of course, the great focus of worship in Israel. There, exactly matching the declared will of God, the annual, monthly, weekly, and daily round of worship was conducted, the priests robed as the Lord directed, the rites and ceremonies precisely observed. And, necessarily, what expressed the will of God on the one hand was intended on the other hand to be met by the will of the worshiper—the formal made personally real by the responsive heart. For (as we have seen) what did a burnt offering mean as, piece by piece, it was fed on the fire (Lev. 9:12–14) unless it also expressed response, personal dedication, commitment of all life to God, total consecration?

Yet, though the Lord was "at home" among his people in his tent, he was not "open to callers," so to speak (Ex. 40:35). Moses therefore pitched another tent, the "tent of meeting" (33:7). This was a place of informal, personal worship. Anyone could slip in for a few quiet moments with God, bringing personal needs and desires as he or she "sought" the Lord (v. 7). The term "sought" is a typical Old Testament word—expressing not something lost and needing to be found but rather the diligent, assiduous coming and coming again to the place where the Lord was known to be and was certain to be found (cf. Deut. 12:5). This is the point of having the tent of meeting. The formal is important: it is what the Lord commanded, both the design of the tent itself (indeed, the tabernacle was also called "the tent of meeting," Ex. 40:2; cf. 29:42–45) and all its divinely intended ordinances, but worship needs its individual space, the quiet, unobtrusive, personal "means of grace."

The meaning of this delightful tent is more fully explained as we watch Moses using it. First, the Lord honored the purpose of the tent: when Moses came, the Lord came, in the full reality of his realized presence, the mighty "pillar of cloud" (33:9; cf. Ps. 99:7), and made the fellowship real by speaking with Moses (Ex. 33:11). Recalling Romans 15:4, that "whatever was written in former days was written for our instruction," we too need to pitch a tent of meeting convenient to our camp. We have a divine command not to forsake the assembling of ourselves together (Heb. 10:25), and we have the public, corporate means of grace that we neglect at our peril—the Lord's Table, Christian fellowship, the public preaching of God's Word, Sunday worship. But we also need the private means of grace, calling on the name of the Lord, reading, digesting the Word of God, spending unhurried time in his presence, looking to him for guidance, leaning on him for strength, living near the cross, turning our eyes on Jesus. Exodus 33:9 implies that the Lord took his timetable from Moses—he was ready to stay as long as Moses wanted to be there. The implication of verse 11 is that the central element was always the Word that God speaks—for us, the Bible at the heart of our private means of grace (cf. Isa. 50:4–5). And may it be for you and me, as for Moses, that "'ere we leave the silence of that happy meeting place, we will bear the shining image of our Savior on our face."[2]

Day 4: Sustained Praise (Psalm 145)

Psalm 145 is not so much a structured poem as a devotional outpouring. Attribute after attribute of the Lord is brought into focus in a torrent of adoration. In form, it is an "alphabetic" psalm, where the successive verses each begin with the next letter of the Hebrew alphabet. The basic idea is to create an "A to Z" of the subject of the psalm (as, e.g., Psalm 119 does for the Word of God), except that Psalm 145 is a "broken" acrostic, in that in the Hebrew text the letter *nun* (*n*) is not used. In my opinion the NIV is mistaken in seeking to recover a *nun* verse (v. 13b) from other sources (set in brackets in the ESV). I would hold that the "broken" acrostic is a deliberate poetic form indicating that the subject is too rich for the human mind to comprehend fully. Who, indeed, could offer a complete listing of the glories of God?

But Psalm 145 is a brave effort. See how the opening (vv. 1–2) matches the ending (v. 21): what begins as an individual "blessing" (reviewing God's excellencies and responding in adoration) is inadequate; nothing less than "all flesh" (i.e., every creature) is commensurate with the Lord's "holy name." Within the psalm, verses 4–7 show correspondences with verses 10–13. They start with the Lord's "works" and move on to his power and glory. In verses 4–7 the power is that of "righteousness," always exercised

---

2. Ellen L. Goreh, "In the Secret of His Presence" (1883).

in the interests of the righteous purposes and the righteous nature of God; in verses 10–13 it is the glorious power of the King in his kingdom, his absolute, sovereign sway through the generations of human history—that is, not just a power in heaven but on and over the earth and its people.

Likewise, verses 8–9 and verses 14–15 offer matching thoughts; note the repeated "all." Goodness and tender mercy (lit., "compassion" and "heartfelt love") extend to "all." And how true this is—although in the throes of trouble our eyes so often lose focus, and we fail to see (until possibly hindsight comes to our aid) the "streams of mercy, never ceasing."[3] But the psalm seriously means its "all." The threefold "all" of verses 14–15, capped by "every living thing" (v. 16) is a comforting emphasis to which we should hold fast. The psalm states it as fact; we may accept it as promise.

Verses 17–20 constitute a lovely crown of truths: there is no war in the divine attributes. The Lord's righteousness is at one with his graciousness (v. 17): it is part of his inflexibly righteous way to be gracious—full of committed, unchanging love—in everything he does, not least in his "nearness" (his next of kinship) to all who call out in need. In verse 19 "their cry" is specifically "their cry for help." Yet his love is not a soft option but meshes with his stern and just morality (v. 20). No, there is no war in the divine attributes. They are all in perfect harmony and unity within the glories of the divine nature as he has revealed himself to us.

Day 5: Worship, Costly and Wonderful (Gen. 22:1–19)

The key word in Genesis 22 comes in verse 5 (a verse to which we will return for other truths): "I and the boy will go over there and worship." Indeed, this is the most remarkable feature of the incident, after we have said everything else—including that God tested Abraham in this way in order to rule out human sacrifice forever. Called to immolate his son, Abraham described it as

---

3. Robert Robinson, "Come, Thou Fount of Every Blessing" (1758).

"worship"! In one way, it stood to reason that this "test[ing]" (v. 1) would come to Abraham—indeed, it might even have occurred to him without any divine prompting. Knowing Canaanite excesses, could he not have asked, "Am I as devoted? Would I accept that?" But the Lord did ask for the sacrifice of Isaac, and Abraham was, as we might say, "put on the spot." He rose to the occasion with calm magnificence. Not only did he act "the next morning," but when delay would have been understandable, he rose early (v. 3). In verse 2 "only" translates as "unique"—not "one" among potentially others but the only and irreplaceable "one," Isaac, the sole hope for the future (cf. 17:18–19).

Worship, then, involves costly commitment: "your son, your only son Isaac, whom you love" (22:2). Abraham and Sarah had waited thirteen years for the birth (17:25). When his future birth was announced, Sarah laughed disbelievingly (18:14–15), but the day came when she laughed with a full heart (21:6), and she called her son Isaac ("May he laugh too!"). What a price to pay to worship (cf. 2 Sam. 24:24). Worship also calls for faith. It involves trusting God for the future; whatever lies ahead, he will work it out. In Abraham's case, preparing to kill his hope for the future (Gen. 21:12), he said, "*We* will worship and then *we* will come back to you" (22:5 NIV). The verbs are first-person plural, and the "we" should occur in every translation to underline the colossal reality of Abraham's faith—as in Hebrews 11:19 (lit., "having come to the conclusion that God was able to raise him up, even from the dead") or Romans 4:21 ("fully convinced that God was able to do what he had promised"). Worship means ever coming to greater and fuller trust, a mounting confidence in God the Father Almighty. For Abraham, then, worship called him to obedience to the Word of God, resting on the promises of God.

From God's point of view, worship involved *a testing call to obey.* Nothing could more clearly underline that what the Lord wants from his people is obedience to his Word—just that (see Jer. 7:21–23). And there is something else. If ever we are tempted to think that in worship we are doing something for God—"No," he says, "not what you might think to do for me but what I provide for you": "God will provide for himself the lamb for the burnt offering" (Gen. 22:8); "Abraham went and took the ram and offered it up as a burnt offering instead of [in the place of / as a substitute for] his son" (v. 13). It is the high moment of drama when the angel of the Lord intervenes. Not your son but my lamb! The center ground of worship is always Jesus. Take our eyes off him, lose the centrality and vision of Calvary, distance ourselves from the cross, and whatever we are doing, we are *no longer* at worship as the Lord would have it.

Day 6: The Moral Imperative (Jer. 7:1–29)

Security was a cardinal issue for our ancestors in their tiny kingdoms. They were surrounded on all sides by stronger, greater—and often hostile—powers: how long would they survive in independent sovereignty? The promises, then, of secure tenure (Jer. 7:3, 7) ought to have been specially prized and to have elicited a serious response. But it was not to be so. The lesson is hard to learn that, precious and potent as they are, the Lord's outward ordinances and provisions offer no security: neither the presence of the temple (v. 4) nor the assiduous performance of the sacrifices (v. 22) secured divine protection. The former underlined the holiness of the great God who indwelled the temple; the latter exposed the sin of those who "came near," as well as providing its remedy—just as, for example, the Lord's Supper does today, but trusting in sacraments is like sitting under the signpost and imagining that we have reached the destination to which they point.

Jeremiah also notes how his people failed to read the lessons of history, as provided by what happened to Shiloh (v. 12). And, we might ask, where is the church that once flourished at Ephesus (Rev. 2:5), and indeed, in many places in Western countries with church buildings that are now antique marts, warehouses, or empty shells? No, the outward, the merely ritualistic, the hopelessly corrupt (Jer. 7:17–19) only serve to provoke divine displeasure—and we too forget this at our peril. The telling illustration in verse 11 says it all: such worship, however focused on what the Lord has given (v. 4), however conformed to what he has ordered (v. 21), misses the point.

Are we emerging from our worship as different people, changed for the better, having made moral and spiritual progress, matured in holiness? Verse 3 says "amend" (lit., "make good"); verse 5 says "truly amend" (lit., "seriously make good"); verse 6 calls for concern for the needy and loyal commitment to the Lord alone; verse 9 addresses his commandments of social, moral, and spiritual integrity; verses 13, 23–24, and 26 bring us (again) to the heart of the matter: hearing, responding to, obeying, walking in the ways and Word of the Lord. And verse 24 offers the sharpest test of all—are we, in our worship, actually going forward or backward?

Four weeks of additional readings on Old Testament worship are available in the appendix.

4

THE VOICE OF PROPHECY

In their own day the prophets were headline makers and pace-setters in the national news. So if we find their books tedious, unclear, less than exciting, the fault does not lie with them.

Isaiah drew a taunting response from the political leaders of his day—a sure sign, then as now, that his message had hit home (Isa. 28:9–10). Jeremiah was flogged and tortured (Jer. 20:2) and set upon by a lynch mob (26:7–11). Amos had a deportation order served on him because his message was a nationwide talking point (Amos 7:10, 12, 13).

It is all very different from our reaction to the three long books and the thirteen shorter books of the prophets that we find in our Old Testament!

How Ordinary They Were!

In one way there was nothing special about the prophets. Those who have left personal testimonies reveal themselves as people with an experience of God with which we can all identify. The form their experience took was, of course, individual to them, as indeed ours is, but at heart they were the same as we are: chosen, forgiven, regenerate, and called.

Isaiah met God in the experience of the forgiveness of sins: "Behold, this has touched your lips; your guilt is taken away, and your sin atoned for" (Isa. 6:7). The sudden awareness of how holy God is made him realize how serious was his sinfulness (vv. 3, 5), but his cry of despair was at once met by a divine response bringing the assurance that his sin had been atoned for, covered by an exact matching price.

Jeremiah was different. He felt totally inadequate to be a prophet, and the Lord came to him with the assurance he needed:

Before I formed you in the womb I knew you,
and before you were born I consecrated you;
I appointed you a prophet to the nations. (Jer. 1:5)

In a word, whatever Jeremiah felt about himself and his lack of ability, it was in fact for this very work that the Lord had him in mind even before he was conceived; between conception and birth he was set apart to be God's man for God's work. Consequently, he was a prophet, not because he felt capable for it nor by personal decision but by divine appointment. God had chosen, set apart, and predestined Jeremiah for this vocation.

Ezekiel, the prophet who has left us the longest account of his call, was different again: "And as he spoke to me, the Spirit entered into me and set me on my feet, and I heard him speaking to me" (Ezek. 2:2). Totally overawed by the vision of God that had been granted to him (Ezekiel 1, especially v. 28), Ezekiel was indwelled by the Holy Spirit and lifted up by him to stand before God to hear his word.

Amos is the fourth prophet who has left us an account of his call. The heart of his testimony is this: "I was no prophet, nor a prophet's son, but I was a herdsman and a dresser of sycamore figs. But the LORD took me from following the flock, and the LORD said to me, 'Go, prophesy to my people Israel'" (Amos 7:14–15). He was a prophet neither by profession nor by training ("a prophet's son"; cf. "the sons of the prophets," 2 Kings 6:1).

Rather, the call of God intruded into his farming life and sent him to the new work of prophesying, to minister the Lord's Word to the Lord's people.

What then is so unusual about all this? Do we not see ourselves and our spiritual experience reflected in these brothers of old?

Like Jeremiah, we too have our place in the eternal plans of God, who "chose us in him [the Lord Jesus Christ] before the foundation of the world" (Eph. 1:4).

Like Isaiah, we have been brought into God's presence and fellowship by atonement: "In him [the Lord Jesus Christ] we have redemption through his blood, the forgiveness of our trespasses" (Eph. 1:7).

Like Ezekiel, the Holy Spirit has come to live in us too: "Do you not know that your body is a temple of the Holy Spirit within you, whom you have from God?" (1 Cor. 6:19).

Like Amos (along with Isaiah, Jeremiah, Ezekiel, and all the Lord's prophet-people), we are called to the task of bearing witness: "You will be my witnesses" (Acts 1:8); "even on my male servants and female servants . . . I will pour out my Spirit, and they shall prophesy" (2:18).

But alongside these basic ways in which we can identify with the prophets, there were things about them that were unique—special God-given abilities that were theirs alone.

Inspiration

While we bear witness to the Word of God, the prophets actually spoke it. It is put very crisply at the beginning of the book of Amos: "The words of Amos," and "Thus says the Lord" (Amos 1:1, 3). This means exactly what it says. While Amos spoke words that "came naturally" to him—using his own ordinary vocabulary, speaking with his own accent, "doing his own thing"—the Lord was speaking *his* words, saying what *he* wanted to say, "doing *his* thing"!

It was the same for Jeremiah: "Then the LORD put out his hand and touched my mouth. And the LORD said to me, 'Behold, I have put my words in your mouth'" (Jer. 1:9).

Typical of his imaginative ways, Ezekiel tells how the Lord gave him a written scroll and obliged him to eat it (Ezek. 2:8–3:3). Every detail of this incident is important, but just notice how it begins and where it ends. It begins with a command: "You shall speak my words to them" (2:7). Note the plural "words." Ezekiel's job is not to pass on the "drift" or general idea of the mind of God but to speak in such a way that people hear God's *words*.

How could this be? How can a human mind think out God's truth and a human tongue express it in God's words? Only by a special, unique work of God, which the Bible claims but never explains. This is why Ezekiel can only help us by an illustration— as if the words of God were written out and he ate the book! Yet the experience was real and effective, for, having eaten the scroll, Ezekiel receives the repeated command: "Son of man, go to the house of Israel and speak with my words to them" (3:4).

This, of course, is a mystery to us. It is a mystery because the Bible never explains how verbal inspiration happens.

English translations have made us familiar with the expression "The word of the LORD came to . . ." (e.g., 1 Kings 17:2, 8), but the Hebrew which is translated in this way simply says, "the word of the Lord *was* to . . . ," meaning "became a personal, living reality to . . ." How it did so we are not told; it is simply affirmed that it was so.

Living in God's Fellowship

We are helped a little to understand inspiration when Jeremiah says of false prophets that they had never been members of "the council" of the Lord:

> For who among them has stood in the council of the LORD
>   to see and to hear his word? . . .

But if they had stood in my council,
>then they would have proclaimed my words. (Jer.
>>23:18, 22)

Amos applies the same truth to the true prophet: "For the Lord GOD does nothing without revealing his secret [opening his council] to his servants the prophets" (Amos 3:7).

The key word here can mean "council" in the sense of a group (Ps. 89:7); it can also mean "counsel," the advice given or decision reached by such an assembly ("conspiracy," 64:2 NIV); and it can mean "fellowship," the close relationship enjoyed by those who share each other's company (55:14 NIV). The prophet is a living person brought near to God.

In this way the Old Testament pictures God's decisions as made in a "council meeting" (cf. 1 Kings 22:19–20). The prophet is admitted into this "council" to share the "fellowship" of the Lord and to learn his "counsel," his heavenly decisions. It is in this setting that the unique inspiration of the prophet takes place.

Tape Recorders or Persons

When we wonder how a mere human could actually speak the words of God, it is all too easy to think of recording devices, as if the Lord used the prophets as machines, overriding their personalities, feeding into them thoughts and words that they might not have chosen. Yet how very far this is from what we find in their books. They are all so personally distinctive. They put things in their own individual ways: the majestic poetry of Isaiah or Zephaniah; the pedestrian, hesitating style of Jeremiah; the complex, imaginative acts of Ezekiel; or the homely talks of Malachi. They have not been forced into anyone else's mold; their personalities shine through, even larger than life.

We must think therefore along a different line. Humankind was made in the image of God (Gen. 1:27). As Genesis 3–4 and the rest of the Bible and our own experience of ourselves and the world show, when the image of God in humankind was marred and corrupted by sin, inhumanity crept in. Adam ceased to see Eve as his glorious counterpart (2:23) and began to see and treat her as a baby factory (3:20). Cain murdered Abel (4:8), and the world became full of menace and vengeful violence (4:13, 23–24). By contrast, the saving work of the Lord Jesus Christ is defined as bringing about both "the new self " and "the likeness of God in true righteousness" (Eph. 4:20–24).

In light of all this, we can state a principle: the nearer to God we get, the more truly human we become. The more we become like him, the more we become our true selves.

The prophets were brought into such closeness to the Lord that not only were they more truly human and individual in consequence, but also they were enabled in this closeness of fellowship to learn and to become the vehicles of his pure, untarnished word of truth.

The Prophet at Work

For the most part the prophets communicated the Lord's word by speaking. Jeremiah 7:2 is typical: "Stand in the gate of the LORD's house, and proclaim there his word."

But on many occasions prophets added to their spoken word by embodying their message in a telling act. Here is Jeremiah again: "Go, buy a potter's earthenware flask, and take some of the elders of the people and some of the elders of the priests, and go out . . . at the entry of the Potsherd Gate . . ." (19:1–2).

Jeremiah's message at this point was one of total devastation (vv. 3–9). When he had spoken his word, he hurled the earthenware jar he was holding to the ground so that it was smashed, its pieces were scattered and lost among the broken pots dumped at the "Potsherd Gate," and there was no possibility of anyone ever reassembling them again. This act was accompanied by a word: "So will I break this people and this city, as one breaks a potter's vessel, so that it can never be mended" (v. 11).

What a visual aid! But it was more than that: it was a separate "embodiment" of the Word of the Lord. It did, of course, make the message plainer to those present, for what they heard they also saw. But the deeper purpose of the "telling act" was to send out the ever-effective word of the Lord (Isa. 55:11) along twin tracks: the spoken word and the visible word—in the same way that today baptism and the Lord's Supper are visible embodiments of the promises of God in Christ Jesus.

The Books of the Prophets

In the books of the prophets we have the word as they recorded it for the future.

Amos's great sermon on current affairs (Amos 1:2–2:16) could not have been preached just as it stands in our Bibles. It would have been all over too quickly. The minds of the hearers could not travel as fast as that, for all of us are like the man who said to his minister, "You must speak more slowly; I am a slow listener!"

In the same way we can imagine Amos using this passage as sermon notes but giving his congregation plenty of time to let their minds dwell on what he was saying—pausing, developing, saying the same things two or three times—all the ways in which a careful teacher-preacher tries to bring his hearers along with him.

But afterward, at home, knowing that what he had said was not just "the word of man" but also "the word of God in the words of God," Amos would have stored away the distilled essence, the carefully prepared written record of the divine message.

Publicizing and Preserving

There may be something else. Isaiah was commanded to "take a large tablet [placard] and write on it in common characters" (Isa. 8:1), and on another occasion, "Write it before them on a tablet" (30:8).

The idea of a "wall newspaper" springs to mind. Most of the material in the Prophets occurs in "bite-sized chunks" that could, very easily and manageably, be written up publicly. Might we paraphrase Isaiah 8:1 as "hire billboard space"? At any rate, it stands to reason that people who knew that what they said was "the word of God" would make every effort to give their people the chance to know and study it.

We can well imagine Isaiah with his "large placard" and can share Amos's quiet glee as he pricked the high ecclesiastical pomposity of Amaziah by publishing what passed between them (Amos 7:10–17). Be this as it may, it is certain that the prophets were careful curators of the word that the Lord had given to them. It is impossible to think that they would either fail to record what had been revealed to them or leave the "words of God" to a version of "Telephone"—the reliability of being transmitted by word of mouth depending on the frailty of human memory.

Rather, Jeremiah 36 shows us how their careful records were kept. The faithful Baruch reported: "He dictated all these words to me, while I wrote them with ink on the scroll" (v. 18). To Isaiah the Lord commanded, "Bind up the testimony; seal the teaching among my disciples" (Isa. 8:16). In other words, "Deposit it all for safe keeping with your home group, the church that meets in your house."

Whether the individual prophets were directly responsible for the final form of the whole books that bear their names, it is not possible to be sure. There is neither convincing cause to deny that they could have been their own final editors, nor any need to rule out the careful, conserving work of devout disciples.

The Prophets' Dates
The broad timeline along which the prophets worked is shown in figure 4.1.

	700s	600s	500s	400s
760	Amos Jonah			
750	Hosea			
740	Micah Isaiah			
640		Nahum Zephaniah		
620		Jeremiah		
610		Habakkuk		
600			Daniel	
580			Obadiah	
570			Ezekiel	
520			Haggai Zechariah	
430				Malachi

Figure 4.1   Dates of the prophets

Did you notice that Joel is missing? The reason is that he may be early or late. The indications given in his book are not clear enough to be certain.

In fairness it has to be said that there are those who would propose a much later date for Daniel and many who would attribute the work of Isaiah to different prophets at different dates. But the point of the chart is that each prophet ministered to his own times and circumstances. It is by listening to what he said then that we can hear what the Word of God is saying now.

The Prophets' Message

Although it is absurd to think of summarizing nearly one-third of the Old Testament in a few paragraphs, we can highlight some characteristic lines of prophetic thought, for the prophets were not innovators but expositors and appliers. It was their task to make existing truth fresh and relevant. Think of it in the way shown in figure 4.2.

Holy God, Holy People	The God of Moses
One God, World Vision	The God of Abraham
Faithful God, Coming King	The God of David
Forgiving God, Perfect Savior	The God of the Temple

Figure 4.2   Message of the prophets

Moses: Holy God, Holy People

When Moses met with the Lord at the "burning bush" (Ex. 3:5), "God" and "holiness" were explicitly joined together for the first time. Of course, when we look back into Genesis, we see that the Lord is the Holy One, but it is not actually stated that this is so. It is very different from Moses onward. The work of Moses is dominated by the truth that the Lord is the holy God, and all the prophets go on affirming it. Holiness is particularly the message of Isaiah: "Holy, holy, holy is the LORD of hosts" (Isa. 6:3).

In order to express a superlative or a special characteristic, Hebrew uses repetition. For example, in 2 Kings 25:15, "gold" and "silver" is, literally, "gold gold . . . silver silver"—in other words, "the finest gold . . . the purest silver." In Genesis 14:10, "full of bitumen pits" is, literally, "pits pits," that is, "covered with pits."

Isaiah 6:3 is the only instance of a quality being stated three times. The Lord is not only "holy, holy," that is, superlatively and characteristically so, but "holy, holy, holy," super-superlatively and totally characteristically holy! The Old Testament throughout agrees. It uses "holy" to describe the name of the Lord—"his holy name"—more often than all other adjectives put together. But when we read Isaiah 6:1–8, we learn that this super-superlative holiness is moral holiness before which sinners stand convicted, condemned, and lost.

Moses taught that because the Lord is holy, his people must be holy too: "You shall be holy, for I the LORD your God am holy" (Lev. 19:2). This was the whole point of giving the detailed law with its commandments. Each command of the Decalogue, for example, arises from some aspect of the divine nature, so that in his law God is commanding that this or that side of his own character should be obediently lived out by his people.

The seventh commandment is a good illustration of this. The Lord is ever faithful to what he has covenanted. Therefore, if his people are to be like him, they too must keep their (marriage) covenant promises and "not commit adultery" (Ex. 20:14).

The prophets applied the principle of obedience across the board:

1. To the way people lived: "Has this house, which is called by my name, become a den of robbers in your eyes?" (Jer. 7:11). A "den of robbers" is a place to which a robber goes for safety and from which he emerges just as much a robber as when he went in. Jeremiah saw people pretending to have a relationship with the Lord, thronging his house, but without any intention of becoming morally and spiritually transformed. They wanted the safety of the Lord's house, so long as it didn't touch the way they lived from Monday to Friday. But the holy God looks for a people growing in holiness.

2. To the way they worshiped: Isaiah condemned a religion without morality, saying, "Bring no more vain offerings. . . . your hands are full of blood" (Isa. 1:13, 15). Even the precious rituals of sacrifice, ordained by the Lord himself, are empty in his sight if people think that (as someone has said) "they can pray on their knees on Sunday and [prey] on their neighbors for the rest of the week."

3. To the way they carried on their business: Amos looked around him at an apparently religious society but found it to be without righteous social values, saying, "When will the New Moon be over that we may sell grain, . . . skimping on the measure, boosting the price?" (Amos 8:5 NIV).

The holiness that their religion implied operated when they stood before the Lord but not when they stood behind their counters!

Abraham: The Whole World

We have looked at Moses first because he brought the foundational, early period of revelation to its climax and laid down the basis on which the rest of the Old Testament operates (Genesis 12–Exodus 40). But the prophets did not forget how the Lord spoke to Abraham and gave his descendants a universal importance: "In you all the families of the earth shall be blessed" (Gen. 12:3).

No one encapsulated this idea better than Isaiah, in the magnificent vision of Isaiah 25:6–9:

> On this mountain the LORD of hosts will make for all
> peoples
> a feast of rich food, a feast of well-aged wine,
> of rich food full of marrow, of aged wine well refined.
> And he will swallow up on this mountain
> the covering that is cast over all peoples,
> the veil that is spread over all nations.
> He will swallow up death forever;
> and the Lord GOD will wipe away tears from all faces,
> and the reproach of his people he will take away from all
> the earth,
> for the LORD has spoken.
> It will be said on that day,
> "Behold, this is our God; we have waited for him, that he
> might save us.
> This is the LORD; we have waited for him;
> let us be glad and rejoice in his salvation."

Of course, there were also other dimensions to the fact of a single, universal God. Amos realized that human conscience brought all nations under condemnation before the Judge (Amos 1:3–2:3).

All over the world there were people like the Arameans (1:3–5) or the Philistines (1:6–8) and the rest. They had never heard the voice of God bringing special revelation as had Israel, but they did have what Paul calls "the work of the law . . . written on their hearts"; they did have a "conscience" that "bears witness" (Rom. 2:15). They needed no other warning that the fearful catalog of crimes against humanity that Amos recorded against them would make them guilty before the Judge of all the earth.

But Amos too had another view of the end, when "all the nations who are called by my name" would live under the rule of the coming David and enjoy messianic prosperity and security (Amos 9:11–15).

David: The Messianic King

With the Lord's promises to David, the Old Testament's great hope began to take a royal shape: a king was coming.

In 2 Samuel 7, Nathan promised David a continuing line of kings whose successive reigns would guarantee him an everlasting dynasty. But at some point it became clear that no merely human line of descent could ever produce the perfect king, and the prophets began to voice a full-blown longing for the kingly Messiah. True, he would be of human birth and sit on David's throne: "The virgin shall conceive and bear a son" (Isa. 7:14); he will reign "on the throne of David and over his kingdom" (9:7). But he would also be much more: "his name shall be called Wonderful Counselor, Mighty God" (9:6).

How the Messiah-King would be both human and divine, the Old Testament does not say. This is part of the messianic enigma that awaited solution at the coming of the Lord Jesus.

The Temple: Forgiveness, Salvation

As we have seen, the tabernacle/house/temple was the place where the holy God lived among his people. Special arrangements were therefore required in order that they, sinners that they were, might live with him in peace and safety and might enjoy his presence. God's provision for this was the system of sacrifices.

The heart of the meaning of the sacrifices (as we have seen) was experienced on the Day of Atonement: "The goat shall bear all their iniquities on itself" (Lev. 16:22). But as that towering genius Isaiah pondered this mystery of sin bearing—how one, by God's merciful design, could stand as the substitute for another—the truth was revealed that in full reality only a *person* can substitute for *persons*. An animal dying can illustrate a truth, but the truth itself requires a person to die, one willing and fit to bear the sins of others. And so it happened: "He poured out his soul to death and was numbered with the transgressors; yet he bore [carried] the sin of many" (Isa. 53:12).

In these ways the prophets took the great foundational truths that they inherited, applied them afresh to the people around them, and looked forward to the great Day when all would be consummated. As Joshua said in his day, "Not one word of all the good promises that the LORD had made to the house of Israel had failed; all came to pass" (Josh. 21:45).

BIBLE READINGS
Old Testament Prophecy

Day 1: Prophecy and Prediction (Isa. 41:21–42:4)

The New Testament is adamant, of course, that through his prophets the Lord predicted the future[1] and that he so controls the flow of history, the turn of events, and even the thoughts and actions of the world's rulers that he fulfills his predicted word at

---

1. See, e.g., the sevenfold prediction that Matthew uses to bind his early chapters: 1:22–23; 2:5–6, 15, 17–18, 23; 3:3; 4:12–16.

the appointed time. This is precisely Isaiah's point in Isaiah 41 (esp. v. 27). The idol-gods, when challenged (v. 22a), (1) cannot foretell the future (vv. 22b, 22d, 23a); (2) cannot "read" the past so as to work out what will happen next—they cannot discern the flow of history (v. 22c); and in fact, (3) cannot act anyway (v. 23b). By contrast, whatever happens in history, the Lord is behind it (v. 25); he knows it all from beforehand (v. 26) and is the first to announce what is coming (v. 27). It is Isaiah's contention that this demonstrates who is the one and only God and who are the pretenders (43:10–13), for to predict and to fulfill requires absolute sovereignty over all the world, all its people, rulers, and events.

Within Isaiah's prophecies, the unnamed conqueror of 41:25 is eventually identified as Cyrus, the coming superruler of the superpower Persia, who, it turns out, is but the Lord's appointed instrument to bring his people back to Jerusalem and rebuild the temple (45:1–7, 13). Now, tell me, who do you see in the portrait of the Lord's "servant" in 42:1–4? Can you name his chosen one, endowed with his Spirit (42:1)? Who is it who will bring "justice" (better, "judgment," God's authoritative decision about what is true, what he wants people to know—his revealed truth) to the nations, do so "faithfully" (lit., "in truth"), and establish the revelation of God in all the earth (v. 3)? Who do you know who has the gentleness of verse 3 with the bruised and broken? Or the resoluteness to carry through his divinely given task without fainting or faltering (v. 4)? It is the beginning of Isaiah's revelation of Jesus, is it not? A revelation culminating in the astonishingly detailed and accurate forecast of his substitutionary death on the cross in 52:13–53:12. Jesus seen in fine detail seven hundred years before his birth!

Prophecy is fundamentally a declaration about God—who he is, what he requires. But very often the prophets actually did this by forecasting the future: telling us what is to come so that we may live knowledgeably in the present and be forewarned and forearmed.

Day 2: Very Ordinary, Very Special (Isa. 6:3–7; Jer. 1:4–8, 11–12; Ezek. 1:28–2:2)

Isaiah and the Sin Offering (Isa. 6:3–7). We need to think carefully as we read Isaiah 6:3–7, for it is all too easy to imagine that Isaiah experienced "purification by fire"—a thing to which the Old Testament does not subscribe. The holiness of God (vv. 3–5) excludes and condemns, but the fire on the altar speaks of his holiness accepting and satisfying itself on a substitutionary sacrifice (Lev. 4:19–20). The "burning coal" (Isa. 6:6) brings to Isaiah all the benefits of a sacrifice for sin, made and accepted by the holy God: hence the accompanying words of explanation—more literally, "Behold! [as soon as] this touched your lips, your iniquity went away, and as for your [actual] sin—the price has been paid / paid by ransom!" (v. 7).

Jeremiah and God's Choice and Purpose (Jer. 1:4–8, 11–12). Jeremiah was neither a late divine decision nor a last-minute panic action. Everything was settled before his conception (Jer. 1:5a), and while he was still in the womb (v. 5b), he was "appointed" (v. 5c) to be a prophet, as we saw earlier. Nor was the Lord's work yet finished: he endowed Jeremiah with his word (v. 11), backed by his promise to watch over his word to perform it (see v. 12).

Ezekiel and the Holy Spirit (Ezek. 1:28–2:2). The "visions of God" (Ezek. 1:1) with which Ezekiel's book starts culminated with a vision of the enthroned (v. 26) and covenant (v. 28) God, and, understandably, Ezekiel fell on his face (v. 28), overcome with awe. This is surely good and right, but the Lord had something else in mind: a "new Ezekiel," alert to hear the Word of God (2:1), raised up by the Holy Spirit (v. 2).

The prophets were indeed very special people: forgiven, chosen, filled/regenerated, and, as we learn throughout the Bible, empowered (in a way that is never explained) to say, "Thus saith the Lord," or better, "This is what the Lord has said," which means, "If the Lord were to come and speak in his own person instead of through me, this is, word for word, what he would say." It is a claim of what is called *verbal inspiration* (cf. 1 Cor. 2:13).

But when we look back over the experience of the three prophets above, were they not also very ordinary? For was not their basic spiritual experience exactly what we experience in Christ? He is our sin offering, in whom we have forgiveness and cleansing and by whose precious blood our price has been paid (Rom. 3:23–25; Eph. 1:7; Heb. 9:14); in Christ we have been chosen "before the foundation of the world" (Eph. 1:4; cf. 2 Tim. 1:9–10; 1 Pet. 1:18–20) and raised to new life by the Holy Spirit (Acts 11:16; Rom. 5:5; Titus 3:4–7). We do not, of course, become inspired prophets like them—that was their specialty and unique calling. But the Holy Spirit is particularly the Spirit of prophecy (Acts 2:17–18), who empowers us to declare "the mighty works of God" (v. 11).

Day 3: The Messiah (Isa. 7:14; 9:1–8; 63:1–6)

The virgin's son . . . the King in David's line . . . the ultimate bringer of "vengeance" and "redemption" (Isa. 63:4)—this is not an inadequate summary of the main lines of the messianic prediction, but the full picture is richer, wonderfully more detailed, always precisely accurate, and fulfilled to the letter in the Lord Jesus Christ. It sweeps through the Old Testament and is the "bracket" around the whole book (Gen. 3:15; Mal. 4:5–6). But just look at our key passages.

He is the "wonder child" of miraculous birth, born of a "virgin" (Isa. 7:14), a correct translation, fulfilled in Matthew 1:22–23.

His birth brings light to replace darkness (Isa. 9:2a), experienced by his people (v. 2b), objectively real (v. 2c); it is also the light of true joy (v. 3). He is the Victor, not only shattering the enemy (v. 4) but also destroying every hostile implement, that is, every possibility of renewed attack (v. 5). He is the true ruler we need (v. 6), and his fourfold name displays his sufficiency for our needs—wisdom, deity, fatherly care, peace: the eternal, righteous Davidic King (v. 7), whose coming reign is ensured by the "zeal" (i.e., enthusiastic commitment/determination) of the Lord in person. Some versions of the Bible try to evade (why?) the plain meaning of "Mighty God" in verse 6, but Isaiah 10:21, using the identical words with reference to Yahweh himself, forbids this. The Old Testament looked forward to a divine Messiah.

Isaiah 63:1–6 is one of the most dramatic pieces in the whole of the Old Testament. "Edom" symbolizes a world at ceaseless enmity with the Lord and his people (Gen. 27:41, 44; Ezek. 35:5; Amos 1:11); therefore, it is the subject of final judgment and overthrow. Here comes not a bedraggled, lone fugitive from a defeat but a majestic figure, swinging along with confident stride. Think of him being asked for his ID by the watchmen on the walls, who await news of the "last battle"; he is battle stained but not battle scarred (Isa. 63:2), who has (alone, v. 5) wrought vengeance, dealt with every sinful opposition, imposed his just penalty, trampled his foes (Rom. 6:23; 1 Cor. 15:25), brought sin's reign to a final end. "Redemption" is the "next of kin" word we have met before: that is, he has stepped in to take on himself every sin, need, or debt that might stand against his people's welfare, eternal happiness, and peace with God. He has "brought . . . salvation" (Isa. 63:5):

> Behold, this is our God; we have waited for him, that he
>   might save us.
> This is the LORD; we have waited for him;
> let us be glad and rejoice in his salvation. (25:9)

Day 4: Acts and Oracles (2 Kings 13:15–19; Jer. 19:1–14)

We come today to a most interesting feature of the way the prophets presented their message, starting with something familiar to ourselves: the visual aid. Think of the startling impact of what Jeremiah did in Jeremiah 19. When he cried out, "I will break this people" (Jer. 19:11), he shattered the earthenware pot and watched its fragments disappear into the heaps of pot-sherds from which the "Potsherd Gate" (v. 10; cf. v. 2) got its name. Impossible ever to reassemble or mend. What a visual aid. Unforgettable.

But it was all more than a mere visual aid, powerful though it was at that level. The incident in 2 Kings shows that the ac-tion of "striking the arrows" determined the extent to which the Word of God was made effective in the situation: three times meant three victories; five or six times would have brought total overthrow. Elisha's action, in placing his hands on King Joash's hands for the bowshot (13:16), should have alerted the king to the fact that he was participating in an acted oracle event—and Elisha's words (v. 17) ought to have put the matter beyond doubt. The mere "three strikes" were, therefore, a dim-witted failure of faith, but they set the situation in stone: three victories and no more, because that was the limit set on the directive Word of God. It was not a superstition; this is the reality of the Lord's Word—it is the ruling factor, and our limitations of faith and foresight and our unbelieving expectations can impede what the Word would otherwise do.

So, then, when the prophets added an "acted oracle" to their "spoken oracles," they were intentionally doubling or enhancing the efficacy of their word, releasing and sending out the potent, all-controlling Word of God (Ps. 33:9; Isa. 55:11) all the more effec-tively into the future. Many of the prophets used "acted oracles": for example, Isaiah used his sons as a sort of "word made flesh" (Isa. 7:3; 8:3); Jeremiah used his "linen loincloth" (Jer. 13:1–11); Ezekiel is rich in prophetic actions (e.g., Ezek. 4:1–17; 12:1–11). But all have the same intent: the Word of God rules events, so let us send out the Word in the most powerful way we can—that is, by both speech and action—and with firm belief in its effectual power.

Does this have any bearing today, or is it a bygone, possibly rather quaint, antiquity? The great points at which we could consider ourselves using "acted oracles" are baptism and the Lord's Supper, which "speak" to us from God. How perfectly the actions match the words: water "speaks" to us from God of his promises to cleanse sin and impart new life; broken bread and outpoured wine, by Jesus's express teaching, are (as we might translate his Eucharistic words) what "my body" means, "given for you." Surely the intention is to "send out" the Lord's powerful words of promise with redoubled intensity, so that we hear what is said, see what is done, and, by faith and perseverance, bring our lives into the arena, the sphere of influence, of what the Lord has promised—knowing that what he has promised he is able and willing also to perform.

Day 5: True or False? (Jer. 23:9–29)

"But false prophets also arose among the people," says Peter (2 Pet. 2:1). Yet how would you know one if you met one? This is the question Jeremiah addresses in today's reading.

Jeremiah 23:18–19 and 21–22 coincide in referring to the "council of the LORD" (vv. 18, 22)—a vivid picture of heavenly decision making, as if the Lord gathered a "council of reference" around him. The word "council" also means "fellowship," as we know, and into that intimacy with the Lord every true prophet was welcomed, to overhear heavenly decisions in heavenly words and bring them to earth as his message. Not so the false prophets, and the evidence is as follows:

1. Their personal lives are marked by "evil" (v. 10), and their energies ("might") are misdirected, characterized by godlessness (v. 11, profanity / lack of due reverence and proper respect for the Lord) and immorality (v. 14).

2. Their influence leads the people into error (v. 13) and sin, and their words are devoid of moral seriousness and direction (v. 14b). They encourage their hearers in false expectations (v. 17),

and they are unconcerned about their scornful, cynical dismissal of the Lord from reverent consideration ("despise").

3. Their "theology" is false, deriving from Baal, not from Yahweh (v. 13)—that is to say, it is materialistic. Baal was the "god" of fertility in man, animals, and crops, the "god" who made the economy work—in short, secular "market forces," the "god" of "you've never had it so good." Baal was also the "god" of sex-based religion, because, to get him to function, it was necessary to display before him what you wanted him to do (i.e., his devotees performed human acts of fertility publicly in the hope that Baal would see and catch on and do likewise): a gross theology and religion compared with the "holy words" of Yahweh (v. 9).

4. All this exposed the false prophets as preaching human thoughts, not divine revelation (v. 21), their own best thoughts dressed up as God's truth (vv. 25–26). To Jeremiah, all such are "lies" and "recklessness" (v. 32).

By contrast, the Lord's "holy words" (v. 9) are as nourishing as "wheat" compared with "straw"; they express and apply to our lives "fire"—that is, they expose us to his holiness (vv. 28–29; cf. Matt. 3:12), for our winnowing and purification. And where our wills are stubborn and our necks stiff, his Word is "a hammer that breaks the rock" (Jer. 23:29).

Peter's warning, with which we began above, addresses us today. The danger still exists; it is still all too easy to defect from the Word of God and, as Paul warns Timothy (2 Tim. 4:4), to "wander off into myths." We live in a daily situation of choice, in an age of declining Bible reading and Bible knowledge—and we neglect God's Word at our peril.

Day 6: A Picture Book of Divine Truth (Zech. 1:12–2:5)

The word "vision" is used by the prophets in the general sense of "perceiving" God's revealed truth (e.g., Isa. 1:1), but sometimes the prophets record what they actually saw. Zechariah 1–6 is a picture gallery of divine truth, and progressive too, starting with the current situation of a depressed city (1:12) and a picture of the Lord's solution (1:18–21), and culminating in a worldwide divine work of "set[ting] my Spirit at rest" (6:1–8) and in the crowning of the coming worldwide Priest-King (6:9–15).

We take as samples the first two pictures. Thinking of Jerusalem's need of mercy (1:12), Zechariah first sees "four horns" (v. 18): a "horn" is a symbol of brute power, and these "horns" stand for the powers that have "scattered" (defeated, brought low) the city (v. 21). But next come "four craftsmen," matching in number the "horns" and sufficient to "cast down the horns" (v. 21). The context is rebuilding the house of the Lord (Ezra 5:1–2). When the "craftsmen" have done their work, the Lord will again have his house in which to live among his people. He will proclaim, "I am with you" (Hag. 1:13), pledging prosperity and comfort (Zech. 1:16–17). The message of the picture is plain: the task of the Lord's people is to obey, to do everything to secure the Lord's presence among them. He is all they need; they must simply get on with the task at hand, trust the promises, and leave the future to him.

The second picture (2:1–5) amplifies the first—a "man with a measuring line." Just think, measuring Jerusalem (v. 2) in fact means measuring ruins inherited from the past. In other words, while the first picture looks to the future, the coming blessing secured by the restored house and the indwelling Lord, here is a man who wants to enter that future looking over his shoulder, determined to anchor the future to the ruins of the past! Did he say, "What could be better than the city of David and Solomon?" Did he urge, "We are happy with what we are familiar with"? Did he caution, "Don't bite off more than you can chew"? Oh yes, it's a well-known voice, but it's not the Lord's voice! The Lord has something better in mind: an unwalled city protected by divine fire (v. 5; cf. 2 Kings 6:17).

In short, Zechariah's first two pictures are a call to obedience and faith. By obeying the call to rebuild the house, they will secure the Lord's dwelling among them, and then they must simply trust him for their safety and prosperity: "Trust and obey, for there's no other way."[2]

Four weeks of additional readings on Old Testament prophecy are available in the appendix.

---

2. John H. Sammis, "When We Walk with the Lord in the Light of His Word" (1887).

5

THE VOICE OF WISDOM

Proverbs: The Wise Life

There is more sheer fun in reading the book of Proverbs than in reading any other portion of Scripture. Its observations of life are so sharp and its illustrations so apt. Were interfering busybodies ever put in their place with such absurd accuracy as 26:17? How well 27:14 identifies with one who is not "an early morning person." And the sorely tried spirit that lies behind 17:12 will find an echo with everyone whose acquaintances include a talkative bore.

But the same sharpness and accuracy looks over the whole of life in this deeply practical book. It is very frank about the frightful "own goal" scored by the sexually promiscuous (2:18; 5:3–6; 7:24–27), and it even sees an adulterous relationship itself—however entrancing it may at that moment seem to the participants—as a visitation of divine wrath (22:14). By contrast, it affirms the delights of true marriage in a refreshingly plain-spoken way (5:18–19). But it is too observant of life to see marriage as a cure-all: things can be sadly otherwise, and 19:13; 21:9, 19; 25:24; and 27:15 reflect how, for an ill-matched couple, the bad can rapidly become the unbearable.

We could explore Proverbs almost endlessly. Very often it just glides over the surface of life without comment, saying and show-ing "how things are"—the exasperations caused by the unreliable (10:26; 25:19; 26:6); the influence that money (19:4) and a well-placed gift (21:14) can exercise; the harm done by sly innuendo (16:30), even though such a person will not forever get away with it (6:12–15); the destructive tongue (11:9; 18:21; 25:23) and the healing tongue (15:1; 16:24; 25:11). At other times it probes more deeply—the accurate psychology of 4:23, the exposure of the too-ready solution and the "quick fix" (18:13; 29:20), the sound work ethic that it commends both positively and nega-tively (10:4–5; 24:30–34). But as we shall now see, there is more to Proverbs than a jumble of observations (however sharp) and precepts (however sound).

The Lord: Wise Creator, Righteous World Ruler

We take the temperature of the book of Proverbs more accurately by comparing two sayings that lie very close to each other in the book:

> Do not move the ancient landmark
>   that your fathers have set. (22:28)

In an agricultural economy, land tenure is the basis of social stabil-ity. Boundaries reflect a situation received from a respected past, to be cherished and perpetuated.

In 23:10–11 the same thought occurs, with a significant addition:

> Do not move an ancient landmark
>   or enter the fields of the fatherless,
> for their Redeemer is strong;
>   he will plead their cause against you.

The Next of Kin

"Redeemer" translates a word used for the "next of kin," the one who has the right to intervene, taking all the needs and troubles of his helpless relative on himself as though they were his own. This lovely Old Testament custom is illustrated in the story of Ruth and Boaz (cf. Ruth 3:12–13; 4:3–10), and the word itself is frequently used of the Lord as the "Kinsman-Redeemer" of his people, the One who takes on himself the debts of his people and pays the price for them (Pss. 19:14; 78:35; Isa. 49:26; 63:16).

So we see that there is more to the "landmark" saying than first meets the eye. The Lord is involved in it, observes when it is breached, identifies with the offended party, and takes action against the offender. This theological basis of the good life runs right through Proverbs. Its individual precepts may seem as haphazard and unrelated as the stones that litter Dartmoor, but like those stones, they are aspects of an underlying bed of solid granite, the wise Creator and righteous world ruler.

The Lord's Wisdom

Following the Dartmoor analogy, just as there the bedrock makes its presence felt by thrusting upward in small outcrops and great formations, so the underlying theology of Proverbs breaks surface in nearly a hundred verses that refer to "God" or "the Lord."

We learn that wisdom is the Lord's possession. We need not discuss whether 8:12–31 (especially vv. 22–31) understood wisdom as a divine person or whether, for vividness, it personified the idea of wisdom. Either way, of course, the passage prepares for the New Testament revelation of the Lord Jesus (1 Cor. 1:24, 30; Col. 2:3), but its basic claim is clear that even before any creative work was undertaken, wisdom resided with the Lord and was uniquely his, an attribute (to say the least) of God in eternity. The same link between the Lord and wisdom is found in Proverbs 1:29, where to "hate knowledge" is the same as to "not choose the fear of the LORD."

Wisdom in Creation

The creation itself displays the wisdom of the Lord. This is beautifully worked out in Proverbs 8:27–31, where wisdom accompanied

the Lord in the creation, in ordering heaven and earth, and itself/
himself rejoiced in the finished product (v. 31). There is also the
direct statement of 3:19–20:

> The LORD by wisdom founded the earth;
> > by understanding he established the heavens;
> by his knowledge the deeps broke open,
> > and the clouds drop down the dew.

But in Proverbs, as in the rest of the Old Testament, the Creator has
a more far-reaching relation with the creation than simply as the
One who originated heaven and earth. He is also the wise director
of world affairs (21:1); it is he who decides the course of individual
life (16:1, 9); and even in small details that would appear to happen
by chance, it is still the Lord who settles the issue (16:33).

The Wise and the Good

It is this wise Creator who reveals the distinction between good and
evil and decides what is the good life. It is his glory to keep things
to himself should he so decide (Prov. 25:2). Consequently, wisdom
can only be ours if and when he gives it, and knowledge if and
when he speaks it (2:6). But he has indeed spoken, so that Proverbs
is able to say what it is that he hates (6:16–19) and to contrast what
he abhors with what he delights in (e.g., 11:1, 20; 12:22; 15:8).

Two avenues of life open out before us, and the issues are
plain. The Lord observes all life and every thought and action
(15:3, 11; 16:2; 20:27), not passively, however, but as one active
in life in terms of rewards and punishments. He feeds the righteous and thwarts the wicked (10:3); he is a fortress to run to in
trouble (10:29; 18:10); he destroys the proud, stands by the helpless (15:25), is far from the wicked, but hears the prayer of the
righteous (15:29). He is purposefully active in everything (16:4),
morally alert to avenge (20:22) but also to withhold vengeance
when to inflict it would prompt sinful reactions in the one who
has been wronged (24:17).

Wisdom and True Human Life

It follows from all this, and from the many more references that could be offered under each heading, that the life that conforms to God's wisdom and to his standards of right and wrong is the proper life for everyone on earth, the truly human life. There are three reasons for this. First, it corresponds with the constitution of the world in which we live (Prov. 3:19–20). Second, there is a joyful match between wisdom itself/himself and humankind as created and intended by the Creator (8:31), so that, in living out the life of wisdom, we are "fulfilling" ourselves, being what we were meant to be. Third, the life of wisdom is under the active blessing of the Lord, as the verses quoted earlier show.

The Purpose of the Book of Proverbs

Why, then, is the book of Proverbs in the Bible? Just for this purpose—to reveal, teach, and direct us to this life of fulfillment and blessing. Its precepts, whether encouraging or warning, are meant to lead us into the life that matches both our own true nature and the perfect will of God. See how this is expressed in Proverbs 1:2–7:

Verse 2. By this book we "know" what "wisdom" is, and we are launched into God's educative program ("instruction"); we come to "understand" (i.e., to see to the heart of things).

Verse 3. This educative program brings prudence, that is, true good sense in the management of life; we learn to practice "righteousness" (before God), "justice" (making right decisions), and "equity" or straightforwardness.

Verse 4. In ourselves we are "simple," lacking and needing guiding principles of life, open to impulse and influence. But this book can give "prudence," shrewd perceptiveness, replacing our natural ignorance with "knowledge," rescuing us from floundering through life by giving "discretion," a sense of purpose.

Verse 5. Even those who are already to any degree "wise" need its help to gain fuller "learning," a grasp of the truth, and "the one who understands" can receive fuller "guidance," skill in formulating plans and plotting life's course.

Verse 6. In this way things that were formerly enigmas and conundrums yield up their secrets.

Verse 7. In all this the primary factor is "the fear of the LORD," for wisdom cannot be separated from the Lord as its source. Wisdom is, in fact, the Lord revealing himself as a way of life for his people to practice. Because this is so,

- 1:29 identifies the wise life with the fear of the Lord;
- 2:5 shows the other side of the same coin—that pursuing wisdom leads to fearing the Lord;
- according to 3:7; 8:13; and 16:6, fearing the Lord finds its counterpart in shunning evil; and
- 10:27; 14:26–27; 19:23; 22:4; and 23:17–18 motivate us to fear the Lord by the blessings that will follow.

But of course, this is not abject fear. It is the reverential fear spoken of in 1 Peter 1:17–19, the sensitive dread of hurting the One who loves us so.

Job: Life Is Not All That Simple!

Proverbs is full of crisp commands, black-and-white situations, and seemingly automatic promises. It would be easy to overlook that it also contains passages like 3:9–12; here is an apparently foolproof recipe for prosperity. But before we have time to launch ourselves into it, we find that there is another side to life, a darker side of discipline and rebuke.

Proverbs recognizes this but does not wrestle with it: that is the province reserved for the book of Job.

Unexplained Suffering

Headlong, Job drops us into life's greatest enigma: personal suffering that is never explained. And to the end, it was never explained to Job why he was despoiled of his property, bereaved of his children (Job 1:13–19), deprived of his health, and alienated from his wife (2:7–9). Job's friends (2:11–13) came to sympathize and stayed to explain (4:1–25:6), but their explanations were doomed to failure because they depended on an estimate of Job (e.g., 18:5–21) that contradicted the Job that God knew (1:8; 2:3) and the life that Job had lived (31:1–40).

Even we, who from the start are let into the secret that Job's travail is a deliberately set-up contest between the Lord and Satan, are never allowed to know why the Lord initiated it to begin with (1:8). It is all one great puzzle, and the fact of the matter is that life is like that. More often than not, suffering is the essence of the problem of making sense out of life, but it is far from being the only problem.

The Problematic Lord: All-Wise, All-Just, All-Powerful

If there were no God, there would be no problem. For example, if we believed that everything happens by chance, we would face suffering and say the equivalent of "That's the way the cookie crumbles." Or again, if we believed that the world is run by human decision and free will, we would face suffering and say, "It stands to reason that we make a mess of the job." It is only when we bring God into the equation that suffering is felt to be a problem, and the Lord's speeches from 38:1 onward in the book of Job tell us why this is so:

- 38:2–39:30: A series of baffling questions touch on the wonders of the created world (38:4–38) and of the animal kingdom (38:39–39:30), designed to show the *wisdom* of God, which baffles the human mind.
- 40:1, 6–14: Job, who has questioned God's justice (vv. 2, 8), is ironically invited to undertake the moral government of the world (vv. 9–14). Of course, he cannot, for only God can exercise this *perfect justice*.
- 40:15–24; 41:1–34: Two horrendous creatures are introduced: Behemoth, "the beast of beasts," and the awesome, mythical Leviathan. These cannot be mastered by

humankind (40:24; 41:8) but are subject to their Creator
(40:19). See, then, how great is the *power* of God (41:10–11)!

Think about it: this is the God of the Bible, all-wise, all-just, all-powerful. If only we could deny any one of these three attributes of God, the world we live in would become totally logical, without a problem in sight.

Suppose he were wise and just but lacking in power, or wise and powerful but lacking justice, or just and powerful but lacking wisdom! Each supposition provides a bracket into which to put every problematic experience of life, for it would simply be one of those occasions on which his justice or wisdom or power was not up to the job! We would have the perfect explanation. "Of course," we would say, "he is all-wise and all-just, but unfortunately—as now—he does not always have the power to do what he wants," or, "unfortunately, he is not always wise," or "not always just." All life would be logical again!

But if he is indeed the almighty God and every experience in life must ultimately be down to him, and if everything is at one and the same time an exact expression of what is right and wise, then we can only join Job in coming to rest, in humility and trust, on this truly sovereign God in his infallible wisdom, unswerving righteousness, and absolute power (40:3–5; 42:1–6).

Faith and Resolute Devotion

This call to faith is the major lesson of the book of Job. The truth is expressed equally beautifully, but more briefly, in Psalm 23:2–4. Sometimes life is green pastures and quiet waters (v. 2); sometimes it is the valley of the shadow of death (v. 4). The connecting link between these variations is the "paths of righteousness" (v. 3), paths that are right in the Shepherd's sight, that make sense to him. To the sheep, life is a baffling kaleidoscope of fluctuating fortunes, but the Shepherd knows. It is he who decides, directs, and accompanies. And the sheep can rest content.

This is the point Job reached at the end, but it is not the point at which the book began. The whole drama started the moment when the Lord's delighted commendation of his servant (Job 1:8) was countered by Satan's scornful yet penetrating question: "Does Job fear God for no reason?" (v. 9). That's it: Will Job still be the Lord's man when every advantage arising from faith in God has been removed and seems to be contradicted?

Would we? Would we celebrate Christmas, marooned alone on a desert island, with goods and family all lost at sea?

The life of wisdom, says Proverbs, can be described, offered as a code and a lifestyle to be followed. Indeed so, says Job, but it is also a life of faith—the faith that trusts in the all-wise, all-sovereign, all-just Lord, the faith that goes all the way in devoted perseverance with him.

Ecclesiastes: A World That Refuses to Make Sense

The third great Wisdom book in the Bible is Ecclesiastes, and what a problem it presents as soon as we open its pages. What a dark view of life. What gloomy pessimism.

Here is someone who undertook to see all life through the spectrum of wisdom (Eccles. 1:13), and no ordinary wisdom at that (v. 16). He gave himself to a full experience of life—pleasure and fun (2:1–2)—but without losing his grip on wisdom (v. 3). He went into property development and estate management (v. 4), acquired a retinue of servants to attend him (v. 7), dabbled in money making (v. 8)—but retaining wisdom throughout (v. 9). And what was his conclusion? "All was vanity and a striving after wind, and there was nothing to be gained under the sun" (v. 11). Oh dear!

Another Ingredient in Life

The sort of material sketched above from chapters 1 and 2 of Ecclesiastes could be followed right through the book. Work is meaningless (2:17); people die like beasts (3:18); mourners go uncomforted (4:1). Would it be better not to have lived at all (4:2–3)?

Virtue goes unrewarded, even forgotten (4:13–16); wealth does not necessarily bring enjoyment (6:1–2). In fact, life is just dreadfully and irretrievably cussed (7:13).

But alongside all this there is another set of truths: when God comes into life, satisfaction and fulfillment come with him (2:24–25); in fact, for all its variables, its changes and chances, life is apportioned out by him (3:1–8), and everything somehow has its own beauty (3:11); the difficulties of life are divine testings (3:18); for all in life that is hard, there is a life with God to be cultivated (5:1); indeed, life itself, received as a gift of God, is good and proper (lit., "a good that is lovely," 5:18). It is true that we have no control over the future and must await its onset no matter what it brings, and nothing can shield us from its barbs (9:1–2). Yet life itself is a joy (9:9–10), a favor from God; the one thing certain about the future is divine judgment (11:9; 12:14), but God has revealed his way and will to us, so that we may live to please him (12:11–13).

Life Is Like That!

What a muddle the whole book of Ecclesiastes seems. One minute we are deep in pessimism, and the game is not worth the candle; another minute life is delightful and fulfilling. One minute we wander and grope in the dark; another minute we have clear directions about living with God and pursuing the good life. One minute we do not know what happens after death—people die as inconsequentially as flies; another minute there is an eternal future and a way of being prepared for it.

But it has to be like that, because life is like that—not the life of the unbeliever but the life of the believer—our life is like that.

Some have suggested that Ecclesiastes is an attempt to see what life would look like without God, the inevitable pessimisms, disappointments, and dark ignorances of humankind without divine revelation. But no, that is not the point of Ecclesiastes.

Its constant cry is that life is (as the ESV puts it) "vanity" (e.g., 1:2; 12:8). The word is not easy to translate by any single English equivalent, but as it is used in Ecclesiastes, it means this, that "life does not add up." The ceaseless round of human history (1:4) and of nature (1:5–7) does not seem to be going anywhere: what does it all add up to? People give themselves to pleasure, property, luxury: what does it all add up to? No sooner is life gladdened by a birth than it is saddened by a death; suffering comes without warning, out of a clear blue sky; there is oppression but not comfort, virtue but not reward, work but not fulfillment.

Can the believer explain these things any more than the unbeliever? Faced with the biting and blighting sufferings of life, its sicknesses and deaths, its disabled and disappointed people, great ones and loved ones alike flying forgotten as a dream, what does it all add up to? Can we, any more than the unbeliever, answer the agonized and despairing cry of a tragic race: "Why, why, why?"

Job faced the single problem of suffering; Ecclesiastes is a wider-ranging book. It raises the problem of life itself and, like Job, has no explanation of life's problems. It cannot reduce life to a single logical system in which all problems are solved, but it does have a recipe for living.

Think of it this way: facing life is like standing looking at a great wall, extending endlessly in each direction, blocking off the future. On this wall are written all the problems and groanings of life, and all its lightness and joys as well. These are the things that await us, lying inescapably across our path. But when we get close to the wall, we see that there is a door. It is labeled "God, revelation, faith": it is an invitation to enter the future under God, in the light of truth, and along the way of trust.

So we enter. We are now in the arena of faith, but we discover at once that the way of faith is an about-turn. We are now walking in the opposite direction of the road we were on before we became believers. The wall is still there, still blocking off the future, still inscribed with all the groanings, problems, and potential happiness of life, and we must still face them and still cannot explain them. Now, however, we are coming to them, living among them, bearing their burden, rejoicing in their joys on a different footing, with God rather than without him, living the life of faith in a world that does not add up.

That is precisely *where we are*, and Ecclesiastes is a tract for our times.

The Song of Songs: "Love Makes the World Go 'Round"

The old song says more than its corny lyrics convey. Yes, love really does "make the world go 'round." The fourth and shortest member of the Old Testament Wisdom quartet, the "Song of Songs, which is Solomon's" (Song 1:1), says to us that in the face of life's puzzling diversity (Proverbs), its heart-wrenching tragedies (Job), and its inexplicable mystery (Ecclesiastes), there is a place to rest, find peace, experience delight, and truly belong—the place of deep relationship and committed love. But why should I try to add to this most beautiful little book by commenting on it? Why not read it for yourself and feel its power? It has a wonderful capacity to speak for itself. There is an opportunity to begin to do this on day 5 of the readings in Wisdom, which now follow.

BIBLE READINGS
Old Testament Wisdom

Day 1: What Proverbs Is All About (Prov. 1:1–23)

Today's reading gives us as fair a sample of Proverbs as we are likely to find. The "big words" in Proverbs 1:1–6 state its purpose. Verses 7–9 lay down its basic position: reverence toward Yahweh (v. 7) and respect for inherited learning (v. 8), with the promise that this promotes an attractive life and character (v. 9). Then verses 8–19 and 20–23 show how life is set between two contrasting voices, putting us ever in a situation of responsibility and choice.

The meaning of the "big words" can be studied through Proverbs with the help of a good concordance, but here are some pointers: "instruction" (v. 2) is "educative instruction and correction" (as in Heb. 12:5–11); "to understand" and "insight" (Prov. 1:2) express "discernment," seeing to the heart of a matter; "prudence" (v. 4) is knowing how to face and appraise life so as to reach a successful outcome ("success," Josh. 1:7)—it is more like "shrewdness" (in a good sense), taking a "canny" view; "discretion" (Prov. 1:4) means approaching situations in a thoughtful/thought-out way; "simple" (v. 4) is not necessarily "gullible" (though it can be)—rather (as here), one still forming his or her opinions, finding the way toward maturity; "learning" (v. 5) is getting a "grasp"; "guidance" (v. 5) is "direction," or steering a correct course; "to understand" (v. 6) is "to discern" (as above). Ponder these words and you get the idea of what Proverbs will do for you.

In verse 7 "fools" are what we would call "fatheads"—people who think they know it all but do not—whereas in verse 22 the "simple ones" are the "thickheads," who simply can't see the point anyway. Both are favorite Proverbs characters. In verse 22 the "simple ones" (cf. v. 4 above) and "scoffers" are those who have given themselves to cynicism, to whom nothing matters any more, nothing is to be taken seriously (cf. Ps. 1:1)—they are sitting on the sidelines of life, aloof from the worries, detached from the big questions, the "opted-out" "know-it-alls." The promise of wisdom in Proverbs 1:23 is, literally, "I would pour out / flood out my Spirit to you" (cf. the Spirit in Isa. 11:1–3)—this is a big, big promise.

It is typical of the Wisdom books of the Old Testament to go into the details of their illustrations, as in Proverbs 1:10–19, leaving us in no doubt about what is going to happen. And very typical is the concluding warning (vv. 18–19) that sin is a boomerang, returning to hurt the sinner—not a delight or a fulfillment of life, not an enrichment but a destructive threat, an inescapable danger, what we might call an "own goal."

Day 2: Go to It (Prov. 2:1–22)

Proverbs 2 is

1. A chapter of *gift* (vv. 6–8): "Wisdom . . . knowledge . . . understanding" (discernment) belong to God. Verse 7 expresses the idea of "efficient wisdom"—the practical wisdom that brings results. In verse 8 "his saints" are the recipients of his changeless love who commit themselves to love him back. For us, Jesus is the repository of divine wisdom (1 Cor. 1:30), and the Bible its source (2 Tim. 3:15–17). From these God's given wisdom flows.

2. A chapter of *effort and commitment*: Looking back behind the "for"/"because" of Proverbs 2:6, we find a demand for personal response and reaction: verse 2—listen, apply; verse 3—urgency, concern; verse 4—effort, determination as in searching for treasure. There is nothing dilatory or casual about all this: a serious intent in our relationship with the Lord Jesus Christ and in our reading and digging into the Word of God.

3. A chapter of *promise*: In verses 5 and 9 the "then" is emphatic—"at that time." When we are first aware of God's gift and commit ourselves to exploring it, even ransacking it, making it our own—as the old prayer puts it, "reading, marking, learning, and inwardly digesting" Holy Scripture—consequences follow: "understand[ing]" (discernment) and "knowledge" (v. 5), and in verse 9, literally, "righteousness" and "judgment," where "righteousness" refers to the basic principles of the ways of God and "judgment" is a proper understanding of how and when to practice them—in short, "every good path." The basic promises of verses 5 and 9 are then spelled out

in verses 10–22 and turn our attention in particular to a fourth mark.

4. A chapter of *transformation* (vv. 10–11), *protection* (vv. 12, 16), and *redirection* (vv. 20–22): This is all wonderfully typical of this practical book of Proverbs. Note that transformation is not outward conformity or reformation but a new inward reality of heart and soul. In verse 11 God's "discretion," or thoughtful planning, is an active force for our guardian care. The "men of perverted speech . . . forbidden woman" contrast in verses 12 and 16 is intended to cover every enticement we meet, whether male or female, and Proverbs is particularly insistent on the danger, or / "own goal," of sexual misbehavior. What might seem the way of excitement, emotional satisfaction, and fulfillment is actually the way of death (v. 18), and irretrievably so (v. 19). Not something to experiment with but rather to avoid like a deadly plague. If ever the boomerang of sin operates, it is here!

Day 3: Perfect Wisdom (Prov. 8:1–36)

Proverbs 8 is probably the central passage of Proverbs on divine wisdom, and very likely the most structured and persuasive. The personification of wisdom is not new, for wisdom is customarily described as "Lady Wisdom" (e.g., 9:1; indeed, the participles "rejoicing" in 8:30–31 are feminine), but Proverbs 8:12–31 is an important background to the New Testament portrait of Jesus (cf. John 1:1–14; 1 Cor. 1:30; Col. 1:15–20; Heb. 1:1–5). In Proverbs 8:12 "possess" (NIV) is the right choice, rather than the possible "created"; the metaphor of birth in verse 25 (wisdom as proceeding from God) is the basic idea.

The chapter begins (vv. 1–3) by stressing how available wisdom is in every place, and we are therefore without excuse if we fail to find it. In verses 4–5 we hear wisdom's promises: for the not yet mature ("simple ones") there is "prudence"/shrewdness (1:5); for the "fools"—those whose minds are foggy (in a bad sense, the "thickheads")—there is "sense"/discernment. The great central personification substantiates these promises by, first (8:12–16), affirming that it is this wisdom that rules the world. By taking it on board, we are therefore giving ourselves the best possible preparation for life today. Further, and more significantly (vv. 22–31), it is God's wisdom—his possession (v. 22), eternal (v. 23), premundane (vv. 23b–24); his child (v. 25), present throughout all the work of creation and world ordering (vv. 26–29); his creative agent "delighting" and "rejoicing" (or sporting with joy) over the whole enterprise, including the creation of humankind (vv. 30–31). The parallel passages (vv. 10–11 and 35–36) warn us to get our priorities right, for huge issues are involved: avoid the snare of the glittering prizes and this world's goods (vv. 10–11); consider the eternal issues of life and death, for the threat of death is meant seriously (cf. 7:27).

The major question remains: how do we in practical fact attain wisdom? The answer comes in 8:6–11, 17–21, and 32–34. As in 2:6, wisdom first comes as a free gift: we "take" (8:10) the gift by listening (v. 32) and hearing (vv. 6, 33), and this requires daily "watching" at the gate (v. 34), where the voice of wisdom can be heard (v. 3)—the verb means "being wakeful / alert over," hence being disciplined, in earnest, not a dilettante. This is reinforced by "keep" (v. 32); in other words, retain in the memory and follow through in action: "waiting"/"keeping," possibly as if "standing guard" (i.e., as dutiful as a soldier on sentry go), regular, persistent. Verses 17 and 21 add the invitation to "love" the wisdom of God. All these directives apply in the first instance to the Lord Jesus as himself the divine wisdom and to our loving commitment to him and his teaching, but in practice, this is but another way of asking what part our Bibles play in our lives each day.

Day 4: Your Choice (Eccles. 8:16–9:18)

Here is one way to approach Ecclesiastes with its unpredictable mixture of negatives and positives, its viewpoint now of pessimistic bewilderment, now of positive faith. Think of it like this: becoming a Christian believer does indeed make "all things new" (see 2 Cor. 5:17), yet we are still in the same baffling set of events as before we knew Jesus, and life's experiences confuse our logic. We still lack explanations. The world around us still does not add up. And here they are in today's reading: there are no explanations in spite of our best efforts (Eccles. 8:16–17), and nothing seems to make any difference (9:1–2); we experience human "madness" and unpredictability (v. 3), the crude intrusion of death (vv. 4–6), effort without recompense (vv. 11–12); wisdom is forgotten, obligations unrewarded (vv. 13–15)—quite a catalog. And we have to say, "Yes! Life is exactly like that!" But of course, there is something more to be said.

First, God is in fact with us in the thick of the muddle (8:16–9:1). It is "the work of God" (8:17), making sense to him even though not to us. It is all what Psalm 23:3 calls "paths of righteousness": life's ways are governed by his inflexibly right and totally sovereign directives. Furthermore, our "works" are in the hands of God (Eccles. 9:1), so that although we cannot now see it, they are going somewhere, achieving his purposes.

Second, life is in itself a good thing, even within its limited scope (vv. 4–6). Incidentally, the language of "perished" and "forever . . . have no more share" (v. 6) does not refer to the state of the dead (the uniform testimony of the Old Testament is that the "dead" are "alive"—in Sheol, the abode of the dead), but rather implies that death brings irretrievable loss of the things of this life: they are gone forever.

Third, it is God's good pleasure ("accepted," 9:7 NKJV, i.e., "with his favor") that we should seize the life we have in both hands: the joy of food (v. 7), good clothes and luxuries (v. 8), marriage and relationships (v. 9)—the lot (v. 10; cf. Col. 3:17, 23). Again, Ecclesiastes 9:10 describes not the state of the dead but the loss of the possibilities of here and now.

And fourth, wisdom is always preferable to folly (vv. 13–18)—

twice over the verses say "better" (vv. 16, 18), and so indeed it is. Throughout, as believers we are called to take up and persevere in a position of faith—the faith that holds to, and lives by, these four important truths.

Day 5: Love: Human and Divine (Song 4:1–5:1)

There are two (very wonderful) ways of reading this beautiful and sensitive book. It is, first, and obviously, intended to set before us human love at its highest and best—and indeed is the Bible's superb "marriage manual." The lover/bridegroom/husband is "Solomon," whose name means "peace/fulfillment/completeness." The girl/bride/wife is "Shulamith," the female equivalent, the girl at peace, finding fulfillment, completion. What an ideal to aspire to— and how right to find it in the Bible. And do note the open-ended way it concludes (Song 8:14). It is not brought to any terminus. This love is an ongoing enterprise. The "tower of David" (4:4) sounds like an unlikely compliment, but it depicts shapeliness, symmetry, the dignity of her carriage. The weapons (4:4) imply the resoluteness with which she has reserved herself for Solomon and marriage. Shulamith's passionate invitation (v. 16) and Solomon's response (5:1) bring us to the moment when their love is consummated—a delight with which they also associate their wedding guests (5:1b) at the banquet.

The other way of interpreting the Song is to find in it a picture of Jesus and his beloved ones, of our love for him, and of our walk with him. Since the Bible abounds in using courtship and marriage (Jer. 2:2)—and marital disloyalty (Ezekiel 16, 23)—why (I certainly ask) should there not be a whole book using God's covenant design to depict his covenant ways—and to do it so richly and sensitively? Hudson Taylor's delightful little book *Union and Communion*[1] is a good place to start. On Song of Songs 4:16, he remarks, "North wind and the south may blow upon her garden,

---

1. J. Hudson Taylor, *Union and Communion, or Thoughts on the Song of Solomon* (London: Overseas Missionary Fellowship, 1967), 28.

if only the spices thereof may flow out to regale her Lord by their fragrance"; in 5:1 he responds, "When she is only for her Lord, he assures her that he finds all his satisfaction in her." And on 5:1b, "Consecration of all to our Master, far from lessening our power to impart, increases both our power and our joy in ministration."

Of course, and inevitably, finding an allegory has led to extravagance and unlikelihood of interpretation, but show me anything that is incapable of misuse—or, indeed, where misuse invalidates proper use. Do enjoy this beautiful Song in all its sensitivity, in its every application, and in its endless delight. Both human love and divine love become more and more precious to us as we read.

Day 6: The Righteous under Trial (Job 31:1–40)

Think carefully about the book of Job. Job's "friends" had a theory about life in this world: that it is governed by a law of retribution. The point is that Job would, in general, have agreed with this, as indeed we would, for we know that we live in a world governed by a holy God who cannot tolerate sin, a good God who loves righteousness, and a sovereign God who rules the whole earth with even-handed justice. The problem of the book arose from the fact that the friends held that this retributory principle was an inflexible, traceable, so to say, logical system of rewards and punishments equally applicable and enforced in every case. To which Job replied (rightly), "Not mine!" And do we not still ask, "Why him/her/me/them? Why now? Why so severe, so prolonged?" Because our logic does not apply. But in Job's case the Lord had already declared him "blameless and upright" (Job 1:8; 2:3), and Job reinforces his claim with his great confession of innocence and integrity in Job 31.

The confession does not seem to be structured but sweeps along from one aspect of holy living to another. Follow it through: Job claims sexual purity (v. 1) even of intent (v. 1), spotlessness of "walk" and "heart" (vv. 5–7), moral probity in society (v. 9), domestic sensitivity toward servants (v. 13), and social generosity and charity (vv. 16–21), following the Lord's own concern for the potentially downtrodden—the orphan, the widow, and the poor (e.g., Deut. 16:14). He has not been financially motivated or grasping (Job 31:24–25), nor deviated religiously or spiritually from loyalty to "God above" (vv. 26–28; presumably "a kiss of homage" [NIV] means some heathen act of devotion). Even the quiet, secret smile at another's downfall has not been his problem (vv. 29–30). No one who comes to his house has ever gone without a meal or a night's lodging (vv. 31–32). He has not been guilty of secret sin (vv. 33–34) or of environmental carelessness (v. 38) or of being a "bad payer" (v. 39). What a record! It may be unstructured, but it seems comprehensive, touching Job in person and in personal life: in society, as an employer, a worshiper, a friend, a landowner, and a customer. No wonder Job refused to acquiesce in his friends' insistence that his suffering arose from undeclared sins!

Yet look what happened to him. It warns us against ever thinking that life will be smooth sailing or imagining that we can reduce God's world to any simplistic formula. The Lord does not explain himself, but he did come and stand with Job in the storm (38:1), and Job found that sufficient. The Lord also delighted in Job's perseverance and integrity (2:3) and proved himself a rich rewarder (42:12–13; Heb. 11:6; James 5:11).

Four weeks of additional readings on Old Testament wisdom are available in the appendix.

6

THE VOICE OF GOD

Instead of Columbus "discovering America," suppose the American Indians had journeyed east to tell us about themselves and about the marvelous land to the west where they lived. The Old Testament is like that: it is not the account of a human voyage of discovery, searching for God, but of God coming to tell us about himself.

Of course, now that we have the Old Testament (and the rest of the Bible), we can go on a voyage of discovery ourselves to find out more about what God has revealed and (always, as the main purpose of the book) to know God and Jesus Christ whom he sent (John 17:3), to "grow in the grace and knowledge of our Lord and Savior Jesus Christ" (2 Pet. 3:18).

Progressive Revelation

The Old Testament is the beginning of God's progressive revelation of himself.

Truth and More Truth

Hebrews 1:1 notes that God revealed himself "at many times and in many ways" in the past. Adam received a bit of God's truth, and so did Noah; God spoke more fully to Abraham, unveiling more of himself and his purposes. He revealed himself supremely in the Old Testament through Moses. Progressive revelation is a movement from truth to more truth and so to full truth.

Some things were for their own time only, later to be set aside. This happened, for example, in the case of the restrictive food laws (e.g., Deut. 14:1–21), which were repealed by the Lord Jesus (Mark 7:19); the same happened too with many of the laws designed to regulate the life of the people of God when, in the Old Testament, they were a political state with their own government. A radical change took place when the earthly kingdom of the Lord's people was replaced by the kingdom of the Lord Jesus Christ under him as King (John 18:36).

Yet even when laws are openly or implicitly set aside, they still bear testimony to the truth. Take the food laws as an example. They were part of the way the Lord insisted that his people live a distinct life, separate from other peoples on earth. This is still a divine requirement (2 Cor. 6:14–7:1) and still applicable to the realm of appetite and indulgence. In the same way, although we are no longer constituted as an earthly kingdom, we are still concerned for equity, for the integrity of the courts, for exactness and effectiveness of criminal law, for social righteousness, and for all the other things the old laws were designed to express and safeguard in the kingdom of the first David.

The Inadequate and the Complete

As we follow the course of progressive revelation, we also see the inadequate becoming the complete.

Throughout Old Testament times the Lord dealt with his people through animal sacrifice and attached real and precious promises to the shedding of animal blood. For example, he promised atonement (Lev. 1:4) and forgiveness (4:20). These were not deceitful promises, for, as we saw in the Psalms, the people of the old covenant church actually lived in the good of peace with God, rejoicing in him in worship, knowing him as the God of mercy, forgiveness, and redemption.

The Old Testament nowhere said to its people that the animal sacrifices they made were a temporary expedient or that the benefits they enjoyed through the animal sacrifices depended on a perfect sacrifice yet to be made in the far future or anything like that. The Lord made promises, and he attached his promises to the shedding of blood. His people believed his promises, and he kept them.

Yet within the Old Testament, people began to realize, from time to time, that something better was needed. David was perplexed that his sins of murder and adultery were not covered by sacrificial provision (Ps. 51:16) yet discerned in the Lord a covering mercy that went beyond what the sacrifices could promise (vv. 7–9).

Isaiah, as we noted in chapter 4, saw that ultimately only a person could substitute for persons. In the long run, with hindsight, Hebrews 10:4 roundly acknowledges that "it is impossible for the blood of bulls and goats to take away sins," but the precious blood of Jesus can (v. 12).

Progressive revelation is not a movement from error to truth but from truth to truth, the lesser to the greater, the provisional to the permanent, the inadequate to the perfect. Indeed, *cumulative revelation* might be a preferable term. The old view of the Bible was essentially correct when it said that the Old Testament is Jesus foreseen, the Gospels are Jesus come, the Epistles are Jesus explained, and the Revelation is Jesus expected—one great, eternal, agelong, developing, and climactic purpose with him as its beginning, middle, and end.

God Revealed

Nowhere is the description of the Old Testament as *cumulative revelation* more exact than in its rich revelation of God himself. Even the briefest review of some divine styles and titles indicates something of this richness:

The Lord of hosts
The LORD
The Almighty (*El Shaddai*)
The Angel of the Lord
The Spirit of God
The Word of God
The Wisdom of God
The Lord Is One

The Lord is many and yet one. In some ways rightly, but in most ways sadly, some translations, such as the NIV, have allowed the literal translation "LORD of hosts" to disappear into the interpretative words "LORD Almighty." The title "LORD of hosts" (which also occurs as "God of hosts" and "LORD God of hosts") first appears in 1 Samuel 1:3 and after that is used over 250 times in the Old Testament. It is greatly favored by the prophets—though, oddly, Ezekiel does not use it at all, nor does Joel. It is very likely that "of hosts" should really be "who is hosts." In other words, the title does not say what the Lord possesses or has at his command but what the Lord is. In himself he is every potentiality and power. In this sense, "Almighty" correctly reflects the meaning—"omnipotent."

The Name of the Lord

In order to introduce us to this veritable galaxy of powers within the divine nature, the Old Testament uses one great name and many descriptive titles.

The one name is Yahweh, represented in the ESV and most English Bibles by "the LORD" (watch out for the small capital letters as you read) but retained in the Jerusalem Bible as "Yahweh." This name had been known from the earliest times (Gen. 4:26), but its significance was kept secret until it was revealed to Moses (Ex. 3:13–15; 6:2–3).

Doubtless there are infinite depths in the enigmatic "I AM WHO/WHAT I AM," but at least we begin to sense what Exodus 3:14 is saying by noting that "AM" means "active presence" and not just "existence." In this way, to his slave people in Egypt the Lord revealed himself as essentially the "actively present God," and his "active presence" was seen forthwith in the exodus, the work of redeeming Israel and passing judgment on Egypt. We will discover more about this in a moment, but for now we just note that "Yahweh" ("I AM [actively present]") is the God who saves his people and overthrows his foes.

The God of Abraham

While sometimes calling their God Yahweh (e.g., Gen. 16:2; 22:14), the patriarchs knew him mainly as *El Shaddai* (17:1; 28:3; 35:11; 43:14; 48:3). *El* is a noun meaning "God," but the meaning of *Shaddai* is something of a mystery. The incidents where the title occurs in Genesis help us, for they reveal that *El Shaddai* is above all the God who comes in power into situations of human helplessness.

Powerful when humans are weakest, God makes and keeps astonishing promises so that the childless Abram becomes Abraham (17:1, 5), the father of a multitude of nations; the barren Sarah becomes a mother (17:15); and in due course, landless slaves possess the land of Canaan.

The Angel of the Lord

But also in Genesis we begin to meet "the angel of the LORD" (16:7–14; cf. 31:11–16; 48:16; Isa. 63:8–9; etc.). The first passage is typical of all that follow: strangely, the "angel" is both identified with the Lord (Gen. 16:13; cf. 22:11–12) and distinguished from him (16:11; cf. 22:15–16). He possesses the divine name (Ex. 23:21) and yet can walk with Israel when the reality of the divine presence would destroy them (33:1–3). Not until the coming of Jesus will this enigma be solved of One who is God and yet a distinct person in his own right, who is fully divine and yet brings his divine nature down into the company of sinners.

Spirit, Word, and Wisdom

The Old Testament has a doctrine of the Spirit of God parallel in every respect to that of the New Testament. A passage like Isaiah 63:11–14 indicates that the Spirit is the One who makes real the presence of God among his people and is the agent of the blessings he designs for them. Also, the Word of God (Ps. 33:6), like the Spirit (Gen. 1:2), was an agent in creation and is represented as a distinct emissary of God (Ps. 107:20; Isa. 55:11). Furthermore, in Proverbs 8:22–31 wisdom is at least beginning to seem a distinct divine person alongside the Creator.

But in all this the Old Testament is not advertising a multiplicity of gods. These are all just facets of the "hosts" that constitute the divine nature. "The LORD is one" (Deut. 6:4), not in a bare, unitary sense but as a great unity embracing an infinite multiplicity.

When they made all the mass of bits and pieces that were needed for the tabernacle, we read that they made clasps for all the curtaining, literally, "so that the tabernacle might become one" (Ex. 36:18), "a single whole" (ESV) embracing a host of individual items.

Thus the Old Testament contributes to a progressive, cumulative revelation of God, and it is the task of the New Testament to "crystallize" this multiplicity into the final revelation of God the Holy Trinity. It is often thought or implied that the God revealed in the Old Testament is God the Father, while the New Testament brings in God the Son and God the Holy Spirit to complete the revelation. This is not so. The God of the Old Testament is "the Holy Trinity incognito." Simply with this part of the Bible available to us we would never arrive at a Trinitarian doctrine of God, but the foundation for it is laid in the revelation of a God who is both simple unity and manifold diversity, "the Lord of hosts" who is "one Lord."

In the past, a person who gave an illustrated lecture with the help of a slide projector had to make sure that the focus was right; otherwise, the pictures were all blurred around the edges. The

New Testament gives the final adjustment to the Old Testament portrait of God, and suddenly all is clear. The focus is now sharp. Everything in the Old Testament revelation moves into place: God is Father, Son, and Holy Spirit.

God in His Work: The Creator God

In what terms, then, is God revealed in the Old Testament? It begins with God, the Creator of heaven and earth.

Scientific research has much to say about heaven and earth, how they began and how they have reached their present state. Naturally, there are gaps in such an account, for everything is not yet known, and it is all too easy to say, "Ah yes, you see, that's where God comes in"—a "God of the gaps" view of the Creator. This is very far from what the Bible teaches.

Two Sides to Every Story

In many circumstances we say, "There are two sides to every story," and this is true. The weather forecaster tells us one story about our weather; it consists of high- and low-pressure areas, cyclones and anticyclones, how they are moving, when they will arrive, and what the weather will consequently be like. This is the sort of thing all of us were taught at school and most of us have forgotten. But the forecaster understands all about it and, charts at hand, can show us where high or low pressures dominate— or whatever it may be.

What the forecasters cannot tell us is why it is there in the first place. And if we were to ask, they would reply, "That's another story." So it is with the story the Bible tells, not filling in gaps in the first story but telling the same story in another way, the story of God the Creator. The great uniformities and regularities that, for example, make weather forecasting possible (and that scientists have discovered and call "laws") are there because he made the world to work that way.

But there is more. Science can tell us what conditions will be like in an area of high or low pressure; it cannot tell us why we are enjoying or suffering from those conditions just now. The *why* of it belongs with the Creator's story, in which all things in heaven and earth are governed and determined by his will and serve his purposes.

The Creation Quadrilateral

The truth about God the Creator goes far beyond telling a story about how things began: that, as a matter of fact, is only one side of "the creation quadrilateral" (see fig. 6.1).

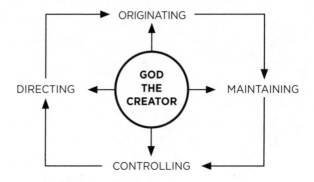

Figure 6.1   The creation quadrilateral

The Creator originated all things, maintains all things in existence, controls all things in operation, and directs all things to their appointed destiny.

It would take up too much space to dwell on each item in this quadrilateral and to give supporting references, but it is simplicity itself to find out that this is indeed what the Old Testament says. In the Old Testament the verb "to create" is used only with reference to God. It is never used of human works of art or craft. A concordance will tell you where to find the references to the Creator and will confirm the truth of the creation quadrilateral.

Such a mighty view of God! So sovereign! So very much in charge of his world! Not an absentee landlord, but an executive managing director! It is not, of course, that the Old Testament denies the existence of second causes any more than it discounts responsible human agency. We see second causes at work in the creative processes to this day in the Cheddar Caves in Somerset or Kent's Cavern in Devon, where wonders of beauty are being formed in stalactites and stalagmites by the patient agency of dripping water. But it is all under the Creator's personal hand. He is everywhere, over all, in all, and through all.

God in His Nature: The Holy God

Psalm 145 is as rich a collection of the attributes of God as you will find in the Old Testament. It speaks of his greatness, might, and splendor (vv. 3–5); his awesomeness, goodness, and righteousness (vv. 6–7); his grace, patience, love, and compassion (vv. 8–9); his kingly glory and power (v. 11); his faithfulness and supportiveness (vv. 13–14); how he provides because he loves (vv. 15–17); how he is near to those who pray (v. 18); and how he is responsive, caring, and judging (vv. 19–20).

What is all this about? According to verse 1, David's intention is to praise the Lord's "name." When, jokingly or maliciously, we give someone a nickname, it is to spotlight something characteristic. In the same way, the Lord's "name" is the comprehensive summary of all his attributes, all his characteristic glories. His name is shorthand for what he has revealed about himself.

But see how the psalm ends. It has itemized all the various aspects of the Lord's name; now "let all flesh bless his holy name forever and ever" (v. 21). This is the supreme truth about him that sums up all the others. His name is "holy," and he is the holy God.

What does "holy" mean? Some say that the Hebrew word for "holiness" basically means "separateness" or "otherness"; others think of a base meaning of "brightness." In any case, as the word is used it means (1) that God is the utterly distinct and unapproachable One and (2) that what makes him distinct and unapproachable is his moral purity.

He belongs in a separate, distinct sphere of reality consisting of total ethical holiness. The mere idea of "being different / belonging elsewhere" is illustrated by the fact that the woman whom Judah used as a prostitute in Genesis 38 is called a "holy woman" (v. 21, "cult prostitute," ESV). She was not "holy" in any ethical sense, but she was "separated" off to a god who was served in this way.

In the case of the God of Israel, his separate distinctiveness is moral and pure: holy in its true ethical dimension. This, in a few words, is what makes God who he is.

God in His Relationships: The Covenant God

The word "covenant" occurs for the first time in the Old Testament in Genesis 6:18, and the meaning it has there remains steady throughout the Bible. The situation was one of world judgment. Note the sequence in verses 6:5–7: the whole human race, without exception, has sunk down in wickedness. Humans, without exception, give God nothing but pain and grief, and a total judgment, from which none is exempt, must follow.

Covenant Grace

But into this situation there comes another factor: grace, or "favor." In Genesis 6:8 we read, "Noah found favor in the eyes of the LORD." We need to be very careful here. First of all, wherever the expression occurs that "X found favor in the eyes of Y" (cf. Ruth 2:10), "X" knows or thinks that there is nothing to commend him or her to "Y," nor any reason why kindness should be shown. While "Noah found favor" is the only way in which the words can be translated, they actually mean that "favor found Noah."

Second, we must note that Genesis 6:9 marks a new beginning in the narrative. "These are the generations of Noah" is a sort of chapter heading (cf. 10:1). "Generations" indicates an "ongoing story," telling how coming events emerged out of what had already happened. When we read, therefore, in 6:9 that Noah was "righteous" and so on, this is not the reason why he "found favor" but the consequence of it. God's grace cannot be merited, but when it comes as a freely given divine gift, contrary to merit and deserving (see vv. 5–7), it produces a new person.

As the Lord tells of the disaster about to overtake the whole race, he looks back to his "grace" relationship with Noah and says, literally, "But I will implement my covenant with you" (v. 18). In other words, he has pledged grace to Noah, and this grace will be the means of his salvation when the flood of judgment comes.

The second great covenanting in Genesis comes in chapters 15–17, when God covenanted with Abraham. A covenant is, of course, a promise, a freely undertaken commitment of God. The promise to Abraham is spelled out in 17:3–8. It is personal (Abram becoming Abraham, a new man with new capabilities, vv. 4–5), domestic (the sort of family Abraham will have, v. 6), spiritual (God's commitment to Abraham and his children, v. 7), and territorial (the gift of Canaan, v. 8). This covenant was inaugurated on a particular day (15:18), the day Abram prepared the covenant sacrifice that the Lord commanded (vv. 9–17).

Covenant Sacrifice

With Noah we learned that the covenant arose out of divine saving grace, freely given; with Abraham we learn that (somehow—for it is not explained in Genesis 15) the covenant needs to be inaugurated with a sacrifice. With Moses and the exodus, explanations and consequences both become clear, for the whole book of Exodus describes what happens when the Lord "remember[s] his covenant" (Ex. 2:24) and determines to do something about it. There are two key chapters: Exodus 12 and 24.

Passover

By the Passover sacrifice the Lord kept his people safe on the night when he entered Egypt in judgment (Ex. 12:12–13). The story, noted earlier, is a simple one, capable of being summed up in three words.

The first is *satisfaction*: when he saw the shed blood of the sacrificed lamb, the God who was bent on judgment "passed over," for somehow that blood satisfied and allayed his wrath. Second, sheltering under the blood (vv. 21–23), people enjoyed *safety*, without any fear that the just destroyer would touch them. Third, we must ask how it is that this shed blood satisfied God and shelters people. According to 12:30, "there was not a house where someone was not dead." This is a verse that speaks truer than it intended. In every Egyptian household the just judgment of God had taken the token but dreadful form of the death of the firstborn; in the houses of Israel (vv. 8–9) lay the dead body of the lamb that had been selected as sufficient to cover the number and needs of the Lord's people (vv. 3–4). The lamb is thus their exact *substitute*, which, in dying, delivered them, the Lord's firstborn (4:22), from the wrath of the divine Judge. Since the lamb had died, there was no need for the Lord's firstborn to die.

At Mount Sinai

In Exodus 24:3–8 the consequent situation is enacted. The altar with its twelve surrounding pillars (v. 4) represents the Lord surrounded by his twelve-tribe people and shows them as "rock solid" in the presence of their God. This is what he promised to do by his redeeming work (6:6–7), and he has done it.

But the Lord's people are only kept in his presence by the virtue of shed blood. Consequently, Moses sprinkled half the blood on the altar (24:6). Once more, as at the Passover, the first "movement" of the blood (12:13) is Godward, to satisfy the wrath of a sin-hating God. But now something new happens. As those whom the Lord has redeemed, the people pledge obedience, and at once the remainder of the blood is sprinkled over them (24:7–8), for, as they commit themselves to this pilgrim pathway, there will be many a fall, many a shortcoming, and they will always need the blood of the lamb to keep them under the rule of grace. Then, as now, it is when we seek to walk in the light that we need and enjoy the blood of Jesus to cleanse us from all sin (1 John 1:7).

The marvelous story of this tripartite covenanting with Noah, Abraham, and Moses takes nearly two whole books of the Bible to tell, but its central meaning is very, very simple: God reaches out in grace to bring undeserving people out of judgment and to himself through a substitutionary sacrifice, and by doing this, he commits them and they commit themselves to the life of obedience to his Word.

BIBLE READINGS
Old Testament Revelation of God

Day 1: The All-Sufficient God (Ex. 3:1–15)

The exodus is basic to the Old Testament. Watch out for references to it as you read; it surfaces everywhere. The Exodus revelation of God included his agelong name (Ex. 3:15), consummated at the Passover and in the Passover lamb; this corresponds to and balances the revelation of the eternal name, Father, Son, and Holy Spirit, in Jesus (Matt. 3:3–17), consummated at Calvary and in the true Passover Lamb. Our present passage opens with God revealed as the self-perpetuating fire (Ex. 3:2): God as life (1 John 1:2), light (1 John 1:5), and holiness (Ex. 3:5; 1 John 2:20). But where holiness as such would exclude, God is revealed as One who makes provision for the unworthy and those unready to stand before him (Ex. 3:5; Josh. 5:15; Heb. 10:19). Moreover, he is the God who identifies with us in our adversities, hopelessness, and need (Ex. 3:7–8): he sees, hears, knows, and comes down to rescue (cf. Mark 6:48; John 14:3; 1 Thess. 4:16). And he is the God whose very presence is the solution he proposes and we need (Ex. 3:11–12).

Moses was aware of personal inadequacy ("Who am I?") and the power ranged against him ("Pharaoh"); he foresaw difficulties with the people to whom he was sent ("the children of Israel," Ex. 3:11; cf. 4:1)—all this and more—to which the Lord blandly replied, "I will be with you" (3:12a), the all-sufficient divine presence, the omnicompetent God, the God who knows the sufficiency of his strength against any foe, his ability to meet and make up for any weakness, his truth to overcome any hesitancy and doubt. He knows he is sufficient; he expects Moses (and us) to accept this and believe it. Furthermore, he is the God who knows, decides, and controls the future (v. 12b): Moses will bring the people out—and (contrary to present expectations, a journey to Canaan) he will bring them back to Sinai (cf. 13:17–18). God is still as much in charge of coming events as when he had walked with his people in the past (3:6, 15).

All these great truths are held within the more than enigmatic name that the Lord says is his: "I AM WHO I AM." The words are capable of more than one translation, but let us be content with this familiar rendering and with its obvious implication and plain outworking. Only the Lord knows the secrets of his name and what it tells about him; we are dependent on what he chooses to reveal. By word first and then by confirmatory action, the Lord lets Moses into his secrets: he is the God of the exodus—on the one hand, the God who comes down to rescue his people in the work he calls redemption (6:6), the work of the great Next of kin, who takes on himself as if they were his own all the needs of his firstborn son (4:22); but equally, on the other hand, he is the God who overthrows their foes and removes them from the scene by a total victory (14:13–14, 30–31; Isa. 43:1–3). The all-sufficient God, to be proved, known, and trusted, no matter what any day may bring forth.

Day 2: The God of the Word of God—and His People (Deut. 4:1–15, 32–36)

In Deuteronomy 4, Moses is meditating publicly on the key events that took place at Sinai (Exodus 19), and his emphasis falls unerringly on the central reality of that great day. Yes, it was a day of terrifying fire (Deut. 4:3, 36; cf. Ex. 19:18; 20:18), but no, that was not the point: Moses said, "You heard his words" (Deut. 4:36; cf. v. 12). The Word of God was the great, transcending reality. About that Word Moses says that (1) it was a complete Word, allowing neither addition nor subtraction (v. 2). This was the error of the followers of Baal-peor (v. 3): they would have *added* Baal to Yahweh and *subtracted* the demand for holiness (Num. 25:1–3). (2) It was a Word with both the personality of its human author and also its divine origin intact (Deut. 4:2; cf. Ex. 19:9). This, however, is exactly what the whole Bible testifies about itself. In each book we hear an authentic, personal human voice but a voice so sensitively wrought upon by God's inspiring Spirit that, saying what came naturally to them, the authors also used the very words the Lord would have used had he decided to come in person.

Moses further insisted that where that Word is, there we find the people of the Lord. To possess the Word of God is their hallmark—and always has been. They did not always have the Bible (that is our privilege), but they always had his Word. Adam had it (Gen. 2:16–17, 24; cf. Matt. 19:4–5); Abraham had it (Gen. 17:1–8); Amos insisted that it was the cardinal sin of the Lord's people to reject his law/teaching (Amos 2:4); Paul contended that the church journeyed into the postapostolic age not looking for or expecting new truth but possessing the "pattern of the sound words" (2 Tim. 1:13) and guarding it by the Holy Spirit—"the word of truth" (2:14–15), the Holy Scriptures (3:15–17), "the word" (4:2).

Again, in Deuteronomy 4 we learn that where the Word of God is, there the Lord himself will be with his people (vv. 4–7). When we follow his decrees, we find the Lord "near" (another way of speaking of him as our Next of kin), hearing and answering our prayers. This, in turn, excites the interest and admiration of the watching world (vv. 6, 8)—that is to say, when they see a people (1) meeting their needs by tapping into supernatural resources, through prayer, through looking to their all-sufficient Next of kin, and (2) living their daily lives in obedience to a supernatural code of conduct, "statutes and rules, as the LORD . . . God commanded" (v. 5), they take notice and marvel. And one more feature of the God of the Word and his people is that all this in turn is the pathway of life and the way to make inroads into the surrounding world so as to "take possession" of it (v. 1): a living, vital church, making progress, advancing, winning. Do you know any other recipe for such a covetable experience?

Day 3: The Hearts of Kings (Ezra 1:1–11)

The Bible's view of God the Creator sees him as the God of the all-commanding Word: this is evident in the work of creation itself (Gen. 1:3, 6, etc.; Pss. 33:6; 148:5), but even a glance at the verb "to create" in a concordance shows that the same sovereign Word continues to rule the whole world. In Isaiah we even hear God saying, "I have also created the ravager to destroy," and, "No weapon that is fashioned against you shall succeed" (54:16–17; cf. 45:6–7).

Now come to Ezra 1. Cyrus was the most powerful man in the world. The ease and speed of his rise to power was astonishing (Isa. 41:2–3); mighty Babylon fell without a blow being struck. Don't be deceived by the fact that all he had were bows, arrows, and chariots. That's all anyone had. He was the superruler of the only world superpower. Like many a soldier-turned-politician, he soon learned to exchange the sword in his hand for the tongue in his cheek and, doubtless, well advised by his secretary for Judean affairs, knew how to say the right thing (Ezra 1:2–3), but the substantive fact remains that he did what he did because the Lord "stirred up [his] spirit" (v. 1).

Like it says in the Book of Common Prayer, "The hearts of kings are in thy rule and governance, and thou dost dispose and turn them as seemeth best to thy godly wisdom." Proverbs 21:1 pictures it like a child at the seaside making water channels in the sand: "The king's heart is a stream of water in the hand of the LORD; he turns it wherever he will." Bible in hand, we can never overexalt the sovereignty of the Lord, nor set limits to its ever-wise, ever-gracious operation. That's the world we live in: his world; and that is the pillow on which we can lay our heads in comfort and security.

More follows: Cyrus "brought out the vessels of the house of the LORD" (Ezra 1:7). Conquerors do not easily give up their spoils (ill-gotten or not), nor easily shell out their riches. But Cyrus did: the Lord moved his heart. And then the Lord went on to move other hearts too (v. 5). We need to recall that life in Babylon was by no means harsh—the outstanding proof of this is that few responded to the call to return to Judea (Ezra 2) compared with the whole populations (of two nations) that had gone into captivity. The Spirit of God, at work in the highest levels of world rule, was also at work at the grass roots. Again, here is the Book of Common Prayer: "who alone canst rule and govern the hearts of sinful men." What a mercy that neither the world nor its rulers nor indeed we ourselves are left to our own devices.

Day 4: No Escape, No Regrets! (Psalm 139)

Even within the Psalms, Psalm 139 is a high point, full of truth and reassurance. Looking first at the end (vv. 19–22), it is an "imprecatory" psalm—that is, it utters "imprecations," or curses, against wicked enemies—and is one of about thirty-five psalms to do so.

1. Faced with resolute, evil, and often life-threatening forces, the psalmists prayed.
2. In their prayers they committed the whole situation (including themselves) into God's hands and left it there (Rom. 12:19). They proposed no personal action, no personal revenge—we would even be wrong to imagine that they entertained vengeful thoughts: this is a pure anger, beyond our reach, not beyond theirs.

3. They were motivated by concern for God's cause and God's name, not personal relief.
4. But they prayed with realism: where we might simply say, "Please Lord, deal with it," they "filled in the details." Along these lines we can understand the imprecations, even if we would dare not pray them. But note Psalm 139:23–24: in praying against God's and his foes, David opened his own life to the same divine scrutiny.
5. Yet the imprecations are part of the voice of God: he is a God of justice, sin hating, ruling in righteousness, taking note of foes as well as friends.

In verses 1–6 there are seven references to God's knowledge of all things, including me and my secrets, my future, my every move. He knows all. In verses 7–12 he is present everywhere—in space (vv. 7–10) and in time (vv. 11–12). In verses 13–16 he rules all, as Creator (vv. 13–15), for he is Lord of life (v. 16), apportioning our experiences, ruling, guiding, planning, wise before the event, our futures mapped in his book. And in verses 17–18 we wouldn't have it otherwise.

How often preachers have spoiled the thinking of this psalm by importing the thought of our sin (which the psalm does not mention), whereby we would want to escape from his knowledge of us, his presence everywhere. This is quite astray from what the psalm is all about: it is a "no escape, no regrets" psalm. It rather asks, "Who would want to escape from such a great God?" He is a God of protection: he has "hemmed" ("hedged," NKJV) me in "behind and before," and his hand is over me (v. 5); he is a God of security, so that whether I find myself in heaven or in Sheol, where the dead live on, or the far east or the remotest seas (vv. 8–9), his hand is there, his right hand holding me (v. 10). He is a God for all circumstances and eventualities, whether darkness or light; indeed, whatever a day may turn out to contain, it is all part of his forward planning (vv. 11–12, 16), and no new day can change any of this (v. 18), for the relationship never alters. Precious truth!

Day 5: The Question Why and the Answer (Isa. 40:12–31)

No picture or illustration can do more than encapsulate some particular truth about God. It is never the whole truth. The "shepherd" illustration in Isaiah 40:11 is true—and delightful—but its homeliness and ordinariness need something that focuses on, and is balanced by, an awareness of the huge dimensions of this Shepherd-God. To this Isaiah turns in verses 12–26: God the Creator (vv. 12–17), needing no advisers, so great that not even Lebanon itself would provide sufficient wood to make him an offering; God the world ruler, transcendent (v. 21), dominating all (v. 22a), the heavens themselves but his tent (v. 22b), "blowing away" earth-vaunted rulers (vv. 23–24). And look at the night sky: each heavenly body in its place, named and numbered, there not by automatic or mechanical or natural action or necessity but because he called each into its position, like so many guard dogs or biddable servants (vv. 25–26).

And in light of all this, Israel had the cheek to ask if this God of such world sovereignty, such personal rule over all, such detailed universal awareness, had forgotten his very own people! So they dare to wonder if perhaps he could not see them or perhaps he had dismissed their case (v. 27). Not so. When Isaiah speaks of him as unfainting, unwearying, unsearchable in his understanding (i.e., in context, unforgetting, v. 28), he does so in answer to the question why. He does not weary in relation to us, faint in his work for us, bypass us in his understanding of all things. We are ever the objects of his activity, care, and thought. He never fails.

Our proper response, says the prophet, is to "wait" (v. 31), a word that always includes sharp expectancy, sure hope, keen alertness, a persevering looking to God with confident eyes (Ps. 123:1–2). This "waiting" brings results: it counters our human frailty (Isa. 40:29) and brings superhuman energy (v. 30). When even "youths" (those in their young prime) and "young men" (which comes from the verb "to choose," i.e., "picked men") flag, those who wait on the Lord "renew" (or better, "put on fresh") strength (vv. 30–31)—not increase what they have already but receive a new strength, different from what they knew before—superhuman ("mount up . . . like eagles"), supernatural ("not be weary . . . not faint"—these divine characteristics make us like himself; see v. 28).

Waiting, hoping, living expectantly, trusting confidently—this way of life involves holding on to the truth we know (v. 28a), filling our eyes and thoughts with what our God is (v. 28b), assured that he will supply our every need (v. 29) and will lift us beyond our natural powers and resources (vv. 30–31).

Day 6: God inside History (Ezek. 20:1–44)

Ezekiel 20 reviews the Lord's history with his people from the exodus out of Egypt (v. 4) to what we know as the second coming of Jesus and the great regathering (vv. 38, 40, 44). It allows us to see how and why history "works" as it does. Its outstanding testimony is that history rests in the hands of the Lord and is subject to his direction. In these verses there are nearly sixty first-person singular verbs. He is the great and sole Agent. The fact that Ezekiel is concerned only with the history of Israel need not worry us: passages like Isaiah 10:5–15 and 37:26–29, or the world panorama in Isaiah 13–27, extend the same truth to all history.

The review starts with the exodus (Ezek. 20:5); then moves to the wilderness (vv. 10–26) and into the Promised Land (v. 28); then judgment, scattering, and the promise of regathering (vv. 33–34); on to another wilderness (v. 35); and finally a purged people (v. 38). Ezekiel is quick to point out a further factor at work in history: the ability of humans to misdirect the plan of God (vv. 8, 13, 21). Each verse makes the charge of rebellion, using a word that underlines the bitterness of their action in resentment against their Overlord: they cultivated other gods (v. 8); they would not obey the Lord's law/teaching, which would have imparted life (v. 13; cf. Acts 5:32); they refused their characteristic way of life (Ezek. 20:13, "did not walk"); they defiled the Sabbath (vv. 13, 21; cf. 1 John 5:21, "Keep yourselves from idols").

But alongside this force of disruption there is the single great factor that holds history together. Paul will tell us that in Jesus "all things hold together" (Col. 1:17); Ezekiel says the same thing in a different way: "I acted for the sake of my name" (Ezek. 20:9, 14, 22, 44). For this reason the Lord did not deal with us as our sins deserved (v. 44) but in ways that prevented the dishonoring of his name among Gentile nations (vv. 9, 14, 22). In each of these verses the exodus is mentioned: in other words, the Lord will always act in accordance with, and to uphold, his work of redemption (Ex. 6:6). Moses urged the same ground of appeal when he pleaded against the sin of the golden calf and when the people refused to enter the land (Num. 14:13–16). Isaiah understood the Lord to act from the same determination to maintain the glory due to his name as against the false gods (Isa. 42:8). And we see the same reasoning at work when the Lord Jesus supported his call not to let our hearts be troubled by going on to speak of the house of many rooms (John 14:1–2)—as if to say, "The Lord who has gone to such lengths to secure the outcome in glory will not allow you to lose your way en route." The God who "came down" to Egypt (Ex. 3:8) constantly "comes" to meet our needs (e.g., Mark 6:48), until that final "coming down" (1 Thess. 4:16 NIV) whereby we shall "always be with the Lord."

Four weeks of additional readings on the Old Testament revelation of God are availabe in the appendix.

APPENDIX
SHORT DAILY BIBLE READINGS

OLD TESTAMENT HISTORY
Meet the Leading Figures at Turning Points in the Story of God's People

Week 1: Abraham, Isaac, Jacob, and Joseph

Day 1: Walking with God: Great Promises,
Partial Obedience (Gen. 12:1–9)

About two thousand years before Christ, the Lord chose and called one man, Abram, intending to bless him and to make him a blessing to others (Gen. 12:2) and ultimately to bless the whole world through him. The rest of the story of the Bible shows how God kept this promise. The Lord Jesus, born in the line of Abraham, is the blessing the whole world needs. Abram was told to leave his "father's house" (v. 1), but he took Lot (v. 5)—we are never quite what we ought to be. But the Lord continued to bother with him for all that (v. 7).

Day 2: Abraham's Family, a Promise Kept
(Gen. 18:1–15; 21:1–7)

God is not limited by what we call impossible (Gen. 18:11). He promised a family to Abraham, and a family he would have.

Nothing is too hard for the Lord (v. 14). But it was not until more than thirteen years later that the promise was kept. They must have seemed long years to Abraham and his wife—but what joy the faithfulness of God brought with it (21:6). Between chapters 18 and 21 we see something of the greatness of Abraham (18:22–33) and something of his weakness (20:1–2). God does not keep his promises to us because of our worthiness but simply because his love for us is a faithful love.

Day 3: A Great Test and a Great Faith (Gen. 22:1–18)

When human sacrifice was part of the surrounding pagan religion, it is not surprising that the thought might have occurred to Abraham whether he loved his God sufficiently to make such a costly response. But when God thus tested him, he rose to the occasion. Genesis 22:5 shows his faith: "We will go, . . . worship, . . . come again." God had promised that the continuation of Abraham's family would be through Isaac; even if Isaac died on the altar, the promises of God would not fail. Verse 13 shows how Abraham understood the meaning of the sacrifices he offered: the beast dying instead of the human.

Day 4: Blessings Abound (Gen. 26:1–13)

By the time of Genesis 26, Abraham had died, and Isaac had married Rebekah, who had borne twin sons, Esau and Jacob. Time passes; people come and go; God does not change. In a time of need he was at hand to reaffirm his protection and provision for his people (vv. 1–3), and, notwithstanding the famine, Isaac reaped abundantly (v. 12). Not only so, but the Lord also repeated to Isaac the great promises he had made to Abraham (vv. 3–5). How odd, then, that Isaac should be afraid and practice deceit in order to make himself secure (v. 7). How slow we are to learn to trust the Lord. How quick we are to turn to our own absurd safeguards. But once more, the Lord does not change: he loves us because he loves us.

Day 5: The Promise Is Handed on Again (Gen. 28:10–22)

In Isaac's old age, his sons Esau and Jacob fell out because of
Jacob's extreme treachery to his brother. In consequence, Jacob
had to leave home. Here we learn how inexplicable to our wisdom the purposes of God are: although Jacob was the younger
of the twins, and although he turned out a person of dubi-
ous integrity, he was chosen before birth (Gen. 25:23; Rom.
9:10–12) to inherit God's promises to Abraham and the world
(Gen. 28:13–14). In verse 20, note Jacob's telltale "if"—the
Lord has promised not to leave Jacob (v. 15), but Jacob is not
yet a firm believer. God loves to be trusted though. The Lord
Jesus made "Jacob's ladder" a picture of himself as the way we
come to God and the way God's blessings come to us (v. 12;
John 1:51). To Jacob (as to us) it should have been a persuader
to trust God fully.

Day 6: When I Am Weak, Then I Am Strong (Gen. 32:1–31)

Though Jacob prayed a wonderful prayer (Gen. 32:9–12), he did
not trust God to answer it, for immediately he set out to win
Esau's favor by his own clever gifts. But he learned that when he,
in helpless agony with his hip out of joint, sought blessing (v. 26),
he became the man who "overcame."

Day 7: The Purposeful Ups and Downs of Life (Gen. 50:1–20)

Much time passed. Jacob and his large family became resident
aliens in Egypt, where his son Joseph was prime minister. The
story of Joseph is one of suffering: brotherly hatred, sold into
slavery, wrongful accusation, years of imprisonment, disappointed hopes. All this we have had to skip over, but we meet
Joseph as, at the end of his life, he looks back and teaches us how
to interpret its ups and downs: "God meant it"—it was all part
of a divine purpose; "God meant it for good"—a divine benefi-
cial purpose (Gen. 50:20).

Week 2: Moses, Joshua, and the Judges

Day 1: The Hidden Hand of God (Ex. 2:1–9)

The Bible never tells us why the Lord directed his people to go to Egypt, or why, having gone, they entered that period of intense suffering as slaves with which the book of Exodus opens. In Exodus 1 we begin to see that, in quiet, hidden ways, God is still on their side. In Exodus 2 we read of the start of his purpose to bring them out into liberty. The savagery of the Egyptian royal house is seen in the edict to throw infant boys into the Nile (1:22), but out of that unfeeling house God brought a princess with a pitying heart.

Day 2: Only God Can Help—and He Will! (Ex. 2:23–3:10)

Governments come and go, but there is no improvement in Israel's lot. However, prayer proves to be the solution—the people "cried . . . God heard" (Ex. 2:23–24)—and he already had his agent at the ready: the discredited fugitive Moses who had been an exile in Midian for the preceding forty years. Humanly speaking, he seemed on the scrap heap, but to God they were years of preparing him for the great act of leading Israel out of Egypt. The Lord, who was preparing Moses, knew all about his people's misery (3:7–9). Prayer is always answered, but in God's time and in his way.

Day 3: The Blessing of Being under the Cloud (Ex. 13:17–14:22)

To us, being "under a cloud" means depression, disgrace. To Israel, the cloud was the greatest possible blessing and honor—God was with them, never leaving, always leading (Ex. 13:21–22), moving to protect (14:19). This gave great assurance but not a trouble-free existence. They were taken what seemed the long way around (13:17–18), because the direct way would have proved too much for them to handle. They were led into a corner (14:2, 9) so that they would experience the Lord's power to save and see the last of their enemies (14:13). God's ways, though often strange, are always purposeful and loving.

Day 4: An Unlikely Leader, a Guaranteed Success (Josh. 1:1–9)

We are now forty years on. Through the sin of disobedience the journey to the Promised Land was prolonged by thirty-eight dreadful years. Moses is dead. Often the end of a long, dynamic period of leadership is the signal for everything to go into reverse. Not so! "Moses . . . is dead. Now therefore arise, go over this Jordan" (Josh. 1:2). Joshua was the most unlikely leader, always needing reassurances (vv. 5, 9). But he was given a guaranteed way of success. The sin of disobedience had lost them the land before (Num. 14:22–23), but undeviating attention and obedience to God's book would give them victory.

Day 5: Responding to the Lord's Goodness (Josh. 24:1–27)

Joshua's great campaigns of conquest are over. The land has yet to be settled by the tribes, but their enemies have been defeated, and the land is theirs. Joshua reviews God's goodness (Josh. 24:5–12) and sums up in verse 13: it has been all of God, his power, his determination. He has kept his promises. But now, what of their response? It should be one of reverence, sole devotion, and service (v. 14). As always, our service is not a way into God's good books but a response to his saving mercies already given. What a resounding example Joshua sets (v. 15).

Day 6: A Sad but Encouraging Pattern (Judg. 2:9–23)

Trace the pattern: sin (Judg. 2:11), divine displeasure (v. 12), punishment (vv. 14–15), deliverance (vv. 16–18), more sin and more divine anger (v. 19–20). This is the sad yet wonderful story of the book of Judges: a people ever sinning, ever defecting; a God ever pitying, ever saving. Have things changed at all? Have we? Has he?

Day 7: A Failure—Like All the Rest (Judg. 16:23–30)

The story of Samson is compelling reading—such a buffoon of a man, never able to resist either a pretty face or a practical joke. A sad figure of whom it was said at the start, "he will begin to save" (Judg. 13:5), and at the end that was all he did: beginnings without any conclusions. At the end of his life the great joker pulled his final practical joke, at the expense of his own life. What a warning of a wasted life! But all the judges were, in one way or another, the same—partial, temporary deliverers bringing no final salvation. The book of Judges awaits the coming of the true King and Savior, the Lord Jesus Christ.

Week 3: Saul, David, and Solomon

Day 1: Another Side to the Story (1 Sam. 1:1–3; 3:1–10)

The book of Judges, especially chapters 17–21, paints a grim picture of people sinking into corruption. But there is another side—a family who kept the flag of faith flying—the godly, bluff Elkanah, with his annual pilgrimages to worship. To him and the attractive Hannah was born Samuel. How moving is the story of the way this young boy came to know the Lord in a personal way. The Lord came patiently calling, and at last Samuel responded for himself. He had been religious, occupied in religious things (1 Sam. 3:1), but "Samuel did not yet know the LORD" (v. 7), and the Lord was not content with less than a personal response.

Day 2: A New Solution—a King! (1 Sam. 8:1–6; 10:17–25)

The life of trusting God is often a strain. Doubt creeps in: he helped me last time, but will he do it again? That was why the people of Israel asked for a king. The Lord had previously saved them, raising up judges in times of crisis, but would he always do so? Wouldn't an institution like a monarchy be better? Then there would always be someone to take a lead against enemies. And the Lord graciously condescended and gave them a lovely man named Saul.

Note 1 Samuel 10:25—all now depends on whether the new king obeys the "rule of success" (cf. Josh. 1:7–8; see week 2, day 4).

Day 3: "To Obey Is Better" (1 Sam. 15:1–23)

In the hand of God, history, the story of human life on earth, contains its elements of discipline and punishment as well as those of divine generosity and bounty. Saul was sent on a punitive mission against the savage Amalekites (1 Sam. 15:1–3). However awesome their punishment sounds to us, it was a solemn decree of absolute divine justice. To Saul, however, it was also a test of obedience. He failed—and lost his kingdom. Saul's is a heartbreaking story: an attractive man with immense gifts of inspiring love and loyalty, but he did not obey the Word of the Lord.

Day 4: Chosen and Equipped but . . . (1 Sam. 16:1–13)

First Samuel 16 recounts how David came to be king, and forty chapters of the Bible now focus on him. One of the most extraordinary things about this unusual man is what immediately follows our passage: a catalog of disasters! In quick succession he was courtier, soldier, outlaw, and exile. Doesn't God move in strange ways? He chooses David to be king and then allows him to become "public enemy number one." Truly his ways are not our ways (Isa. 55:8). David has a hard road to tread and difficult lessons of trust to learn.

Day 5: Touching Bottom (1 Sam. 30:1–6; 2 Sam. 2:1–7)

Poor David. In all the miseries of exile there was one place to call home—Ziklag. But he returned to find it a heap of ruins, his family captured, and his devoted followers ready to kill him. How do we react to such a blow? "David strengthened himself in the Lord his God" (1 Sam. 30:6). Then he found it to be true (Ps. 113:7–8) that the distance from the ash heap to the throne is short (2 Sam. 2:7)—a king at last. The Lord who brings down, brings up; not until we have been brought low can we be entrusted with the heights.

Day 6: David's Everlasting House (2 Sam. 7:1–22)

How can we read 2 Samuel 7 without reaching forward to Luke 1:30–33, where the story ends? How marvelous are God's ways! David, of course, did not know all this, but he was overwhelmed with gratitude for what he did know: he set out to build a house for the Lord only to find that the Lord planned to build a lasting royal house for him. In its way this is what the Old Testament is all about—the search and the wait for the perfect King. And now he has come: the Lord Jesus Christ.

Day 7: Another Brilliant Failure (1 Kings 3:1–15; 11:1–6)

The Old Testament never did find the perfect king, not even in Solomon. Truly the Lord gave him unique wisdom, and as with all God's gifts, along with it came those things that would test it. Would he develop the character to sustain his wisdom in the face of the testings of wealth, the applause of people ("honor," 1 Kings 3:13), and the tendency of old men to become old fools? No king ever had such a chance to be the perfect king, and none collapsed so signally. With the Old Testament examples before us, we know that our salvation cannot be in man. We need someone greater than Solomon (Matt. 12:42).

Week 4: King after King, Kings of All Sorts, Human Failure

Day 1: Goodbye, David (1 Kings 12:1–20)

What destroyed Rehoboam? In a word, arrogance. He couldn't be told. The story of Solomon shows that human character cannot stand life's testings. Rehoboam tells us that youthful assurance is not the answer either. Solomon the wise fell to folly; Rehoboam the confident fell to overconfidence. These kings teach us self-distrust; they are mirrors of the human heart. It is not "There but for the grace of God go I," but simply "There go I." May the revelation of weakness drive us to seek God's grace.

Day 2: It Is Not Enough to Be Gifted (2 Kings 9:1–28)

Following the disastrous Rehoboam, David's kingdom split into two: the ten tribes of Israel (or Ephraim) to the north and the two tribes of Judah to the south. The northern kings raised themselves to the throne by their natural gifts: ambitious, able men aiming for the top. Jehu is typical: a brilliant commander (see how readily his peers offer him loyalty, 2 Kings 9:13), but what a ruthless brute of a man. No salvation for God's people here.

Day 3: It Is Not Even Enough to Reform (2 Kings 22:1–13; 23:24–26)

Josiah is typical of the best of the south. Born in David's line, inheritor and custodian of the Lord's promises to David, he was well set for success by the discovery of the lost book. Now the kingdom could be governed by God's Word. But what about the past? Before the good Josiah, his terrible father, Manasseh, had dropped a brick into the pool of history; Josiah rectified much of his father's error, but he could not hold back the swelling ripples in the pool (2 Kings 23:26). The people of God need a king who can deal with their past as well as their present and future. Only Jesus is such a King.

Day 4: Name without Reality (2 Kings 24:18–25:21)

Zedekiah means "The Lord is [my] righteousness," but the king was not that sort of man at all. He "did what was evil in the sight of the Lord" (2 Kings 24:19), and that, to the Lord, was the last straw. We cannot read the story of the destruction of old Jerusalem without a pang of sadness—all the glory of David and Solomon brought to the dust. But we must face the truth, and the Old Testament is there to teach it to us, that we must not deceive ourselves. God is not mocked; what people sow, they reap (Gal. 6:7). Not even precious Jerusalem, the city that the Lord himself chose, is immune from this dread law.

Day 5: A Movement of the Heart (Ezra 1:1–11)

Seventy years have passed since Jerusalem was destroyed. The Lord's people are exiles (but otherwise not greatly oppressed) in Babylon. They cannot have heard with equanimity, in the years prior to 539 BC, that a greater conqueror, Cyrus, was on his way. Surely this could only spell further bondage and prolonged exile. To think like this is to reckon without God. He is the Lord of all hearts (Ezra 1:1, 5).

Day 6: First Things First (Ezra 3:1–13)

Try to feel the excitement of the returned community: back home and the great day of festal gathering to recommence worship! What was their first commitment? To obey the Word of the Lord (Ezra 3:2, 4–5): all must be done as it is written, required, and appointed. What was their first act? To set up the altar (v. 2). The temple area was not yet cleared of rubble, the house itself not yet rebuilt, but first they set up the altar, the place where the atoning sacrifices were made; first and foremost is the need to be right with God through the blood sacrifices he has appointed.

Day 7: Another "First Thing" First (Neh. 1:1–11)

The Persian Empire is now supreme in all lands. Nehemiah, in far-off Susa, learns from eyewitnesses how desolate Jerusalem is, and the Lord stirs his heart to put things right. No small undertaking for a courtier to turn builder! So what did he do first? He made use of the often neglected, frequently despised power of prayer, and according to the dates given in his book (Neh. 1:1; 2:1), the Lord kept him at his prayers for three months before opening the door of opportunity to speak to the king. It is not a bad point at which to conclude our tour: a praying man, looking forward to the city of God.

OLD TESTAMENT RELIGION
Meet the Church in Its Public Religious Observances and Its Members as They Walked with God

Week 1: The Holy God Living among His People
Day 1: A Lovely Divine Purpose (Ex. 29:42–46)

Up to this point the book of Exodus has made three things plain: (1) with patience and power the Lord brought his people out of Egyptian slavery; (2) there was little that was attractive about them—they resisted his word, grumbled at his ways, and even regretted that he had brought them out at all; and (3) the tent (tabernacle) in which God wished to dwell is described by God in great detail (Exodus 25–31). This tent, says today's passage (29:42–46), was the very reason why he brought them out and bore with them, so that he might dwell among them. They were a people in tents, so he would be a camping God with his tent among theirs. He is a God near at hand, sharing our lot, bearing with our oddities, available for our needs (Eph. 2:19–22).

Day 2: Still the Same: The Lord among His People
(2 Sam. 7:1–3, 12–13)

Four hundred years have passed, but God remains the same. David is now on the throne, and his instincts tell him, correctly, that the God who lived in a mobile home, when his people were traveling people, would now wish to have his house among their houses. No wonder Nathan promptly agreed: the Lord the Bible reveals is always the indwelling Lord, at hand, with and among us. But he is still the Lord: he does things his way, and the time is not yet right (read 2 Sam.7:9 with Deut. 12:10–11), and the man is not right (read 2 Sam. 7:5 with 1 Chron. 22:8—the man of war cannot build the house of peace). But by all this we see that it is not man's will to provide a house and (so to speak) "organize" the Lord's presence with us; it is his will that he should come to live where we live.

Day 3: Very Wonderful, Very True (1 Kings 8:12–13, 17–21, 27–29)

Note the central thought in each short passage. (1) First Kings 8:12–13: What is the house for? The God whom we could never discover or find for ourselves (hidden in thick darkness) comes to live among his people. (2) Verses 17–21: It is his purpose to do so; that is why he kept his promise to give David a son and heir. His "name" (v. 20) is shorthand for "all that the Lord has revealed about himself"; that is, God in the fullness of his revealed character comes to dwell in the house. (3) Verses 27–29: Yes, he really does. The heavens are too small to contain his greatness, yet he has undertaken that his "name" will dwell in the house. He will fully and truly live "down among" his people.

Day 4: Strange—but It Stands to Reason! (Ex. 40:34–38)

In the book of Exodus, all the details of the Lord's tent are given twice over. First, everything is described (chaps. 25–31), and then everything is done as described (chaps. 35–40). Finally, the day came when everything was exactly right, just as the Lord wished it, and true to his word, he came visibly in the cloud, signifying that "God is here" to take up residence among his people. But not even Moses could enter where the Lord was (40:35). The Lord was at home, but not "at home" to callers. For when he comes, he comes as he is, in all the fullness of his holy nature, and how could we possibly enter and come before the Holy One? We can't. It stands to reason.

Day 5: Moses's Experience: Shut Out . . . Let In (Ex. 3:15)

What a vivid scene. The flame of fire in the bush. A unique flame that needed no fuel to feed on: the bush was only the dwelling place of a flame that was self-sufficient, full of life all its own. The voice from the bush explained that this represented the threatening holiness of God, which Moses dare not approach. As we saw in yesterday's reading, the Lord's holiness is not a passive beauty but an active force that threatens and excludes all that offends it. But here is something wonderful: Moses is told a simple thing to do whereby he will be safe and accepted. Take off his shoes. As we shall learn, this too is true of the God of the Bible: it is like him to make a simple provision whereby we can enter and enjoy the fellowship of the Holy One (see John 14:6).

Day 6: Isaiah's Experience: A Threatening Holiness (Isa. 6:1–5)

Uzziah had reigned for fifty-two years. As the old king's life slipped away, was Isaiah comforted by the thought that though kings have to go, the King (Isa. 6:1, "the Lord," or "the Sovereign") remains? If so, the comfort soon passed, for the seraphim were proclaiming the holiness of God. The Hebrew repeats a word in order to emphasize it. This is the only case where an attribute is stated three times: the holiness of the Lord is super-superlative! It is a sobering thought that a sin we might have dismissed as pretty negligible, a sin of speech, blots out the vision of God and prompts Isaiah's conviction that he is doomed.

Day 7: Isaiah's Experience: The Way Home to God (Isa. 6:6–8)

When the cloud blotted out everything else, the altar and its flaming embers remained in view. The coal, which was pressed to the place where Isaiah knew himself to be a sinner, represented all that the altar stood for—a sacrifice to God making atonement, covering our sin, bringing forgiveness and reconciliation. The words of the seraph explain this: iniquity and sin are taken away, the price has been paid, and Isaiah, who first saw the Lord only far off (Isa. 6:1) and then was excluded from his presence altogether (vv. 4–5), is now, because forgiven, brought into his close fellowship, into a speaking relationship with the holy God.

Week 2: "Not without Blood": The Sacrifices and Their Meaning

Day 1: The Carefully Selected Lamb (Ex. 12:1–6)

The people were slaves in Egypt, doomed to death. The Lord's command to "take a lamb" (Ex. 12:3) could well have seemed totally irrelevant, but it was in fact the key to their redemption and freedom. The Lord had promised not only to bring them out *from* Egypt but also to bring them *to* himself (6:6–7), for there is no true freedom unless people are at peace with God. As a first step he required them to select a lamb very carefully so that it exactly represented the number and the needs of the people of God (12:4). Its "perfection" made it acceptable to God (v. 5). This was the lamb that was destined to die (v. 6).

Day 2: Peace with God (Ex. 12:7–13)

Every verse in the Exodus 12:7–13 passage is important, but most of all verse 13. The blood of the lamb (symbolizing its death) has been sprinkled (v. 7). The people are inside the blood-marked houses and are at the ready, dressed for the journey (v. 11). The Lord enters Egypt as Judge and Executioner (v. 12) but, seeing the blood, has no case to pursue or judgment to execute against those sheltering there (v. 13). Is it daring to say that the blood "changes" God? The fact is that when he sees the blood, wrath is gone, and he "passes over" in peace. This is what John meant when he pointed to Jesus as "the Lamb of God" (John 1:29, 36), and what Paul meant when he said we have peace with God through "the blood of his cross" (Col. 1:20).

Day 3: The Sheltered People (Ex. 12:21–24)

Exodus 12:21–24 emphasizes what we already know from verse 13. Those who have entered where the blood of the lamb was shed are safe. Note how verses 22–23 keep coming back to "the blood"—that is the vital matter. The lamb has died, and as we saw on day 1, the lamb was equivalent to the number and needs of the people on the one hand and, in its perfection, was acceptable to God on the other. The holy Judge is satisfied when the lamb, equivalent to his people, has died. What the Passover depicts in this way is the central truth of the Bible (not just the Old Testament) about atonement and peace with God. In the wise and merciful plan of God, the perfect dies in the place of the needy so that we may enjoy peace with a satisfied God.

Day 4: Making Atonement: The Unseen Reality (Lev. 16:15–17)

In the tent (tabernacle) in which the Lord lived among his people, the inner shrine was only entered once a year. On the Day of Atonement the high priest brought in there the blood of the sin offering and sprinkled it before God, making atonement "for himself and for his house and for all the assembly of Israel" (Lev. 16:17). In this way the people brought proof to God that the beast designated as a sin offering had died, and God accepted this death as paying for and thus covering all the sins of the people throughout the preceding year. "Atonement" literally means "covering," not simply in the sense of hiding away but in the sense that payment "covers" a debt—paying and canceling.

Day 5: The Sin Bearer, the Visible Demonstration (Lev. 16:20–22)

The Lord wanted his people to know what it was that had happened in the secrecy of the inner shrine, so a second and public ceremony was appointed. When Aaron laid his hands on the chosen beast and confessed Israel's sins, we read that he put them on the head of the goat (Lev. 16:21) and that the goat bore all their iniquities away—a vivid picture of the innocent taking the place of the guilty, accepting their offenses as his own, and bearing them away never to be seen again. This is what all the atoning sacrifices meant: they were substitutionary (one taking the place of another) and sin bearing (one accepting and removing the sin of another). In every case the payment was a life laid down. The Lord Jesus himself taught us to understand his death in exactly this way (Mark 10:45). Consequently, this is how the New Testament understands the cross (e.g., 1 Tim. 2:5–6; 1 Pet. 2:24; 3:18).

Day 6: The Offering That Holds Nothing Back (Lev. 1:3–9)

Besides the sin offering, one of the main offerings appointed by God was the burnt offering. When Abraham was called to offer Isaac, it was as a burnt offering (Gen. 22:2). His readiness to do so proved that he had "not withheld" anything God required (v. 12). Like all the offerings, this involved (1) laying hands on the animal, that is, appointing the animal as a substitute (see day 5); (2) making atonement by presenting the blood (Lev. 1:5); and (3) offering the entire beast as a sacrifice to God (v. 9). This means that when we belong to God by atonement, he looks to us to hold nothing back in our devoted obedience to him.

Day 7: A Shared Joy (Lev. 3:12–16; 7:11–15)

The third of the main offerings was the peace, or fellowship, offering. It was made on occasions of joy or thanksgiving or as an act of special devotion to the Lord. Part of it was burned, and this is called "food" (Lev. 3:16)—not as if they were feeding God but to symbolize the fact that he came himself to share in his people's joy. Part was given to the priest (7:14), and the remainder was enjoyed by the worshiper that day—a command that necessitated inviting others to the party (Deut. 16:11), for who alone could eat the rest of a whole beast? This sacrifice involved personal, familial, and communal joy, resting on and arising out of atonement, peace with God.

Week 3: Ritual and Response, Religion and Holiness

Day 1: Only the Best for the Lord (Mal. 1:6–10)

Malachi's topic is plain enough: it is so easy to come to regard religious observance as an end in itself, especially with a religion like that of the Old Testament, where so many rituals were obligatory. Malachi's people had fallen into the snare of thinking that somehow these rituals, simply as performances, were pleasing to the Lord. But it is never so. Ceremonies impose demands on the worshiper, for religious observance begins in the heart. Since actions speak louder than words, it was the way they behaved that showed that they despised his name and said his table was contemptible. But the Lord would rather not have the ritual than have it without the heart's devotion and commitment of his people.

Day 2: No Benefit without Commitment (Jer. 7:4–11)

The temple and its services were ordained by God (Jer. 7:4), but Jeremiah found people thinking that just because the temple stood there and its services were performed, they were somehow safe from every threat; they were keeping themselves in God's good books. But there is no true religion without mending our ways (v. 5). They were in fact treating the Lord's house as robbers treat their "den" (v. 11), a place to go to for safety and then come out from it every bit as much robbers and villains as when they went in. When we think of the main offerings noted in last week's readings, what is the point of the sin offering without repentance and hatred of sin? Or of the burnt offering without "holding nothing back" from God?

Day 3: Keeping the Balance Right (Amos 5:21–25)

It must have sounded simply dreadful to hear Amos say that the Lord hated the religious services that he had himself ordained: feasts, gatherings, offerings, worship—all detestable! And so they are if they are divorced from living justly and righteously (Amos 5:24). The question in verse 25 implies, "Was it *sacrifices* you brought me? Was that *all*?" Yes indeed, they had brought sacrifices, but they had also brought obedience to the Lord's law given at Sinai. Religion went hand in hand with obedience to God's Word. The truths of these three days' readings are for us too. The religion of the Bible is all of a piece. We have our God-ordained services and worship. Sadly, we too can become slipshod and second rate (day 1), lacking moral commitment (day 2), and forgetful of the balance between the means of grace and the responsive life of obedience (day 3).

Day 4: A Picture of the True (Ex. 24:4–8)

The picture in Exodus 24:4 is self-explanatory: the Lord has kept his promise of Exodus 6:6–7. He has gathered his people into his presence. Moses sprinkles the blood on the altar (24:6) because it is the sprinkled blood that makes peace with God. Only around a bloodstained altar are the Lord's people in fellowship with him. But watch what happens next: (1) those who are at peace with God are called to hear his Word and obey it (v. 7); (2) because our obedience at best is a patchy affair with many false starts, many slips, and much left undone, we need the cleansing blood as our constant covering (v. 8). See 1 John 1:7—as we "walk" (our daily life of obedience) in his way, the blood of Jesus goes on cleansing us.

Day 5: The Way of Repentance (Ps. 32:1–7)

Psalm 32 does not specifically link itself with the time when David committed adultery with Bathsheba and secured the death of her husband, but verse 5 is the perfect poetic counterpart of 2 Samuel 12:13. God's law provided no atoning sacrifice for adultery and murder, only the death penalty. But David found that if he truly repented, even these sins could be forgiven. This is the effectiveness of simple penitence. By this means we enter into forgiveness (Ps. 32:1), a clear account before God (v. 2), and the misery of the sinner (v. 3) is replaced by the song of one who has been delivered (v. 7).

Day 6: The Way of Obedience (Isa. 1:11–20)

Once more a prophet exposes the hollowness before God of a "prayer wheel" religion—keeping the ritual in motion while neglecting personal holiness. In their gatherings the Lord saw an unholy mixture (lit., "wickedness along with religious dutifulness," Isa. 1:13); when they prayed, he could not hear the words they said because he was looking at their hands, stained with many an uncleansed, unrepented sin (v. 15). But the remedy was available: in verse 16 the first verb, "wash," implies "make use of the religious ceremonies of purification"; the second verb, "make . . . clean," means "bring about a moral reformation"—the life of obedience to God's Word (v. 19). Obeying him is the proper outcome of his offer of cleansing (v. 18).

Day 7: The Enduring Foundation (Amos 7:7–9)

The wall Amos saw is the wall of our life as we have been, and are, building it. "Built with a plumb line" (Amos 7:7) means that the plumb line was available to the builder all day long. But it is now to be tested by the Lord's plumb line. From the start of building, the people had (as we have) both God's law to obey and God's grace to cleanse (see day 4). The true, God-intended life of the Lord's people (then and now) stands straight and firm when it rests always on his forgiving grace and is committed to obeying his holy law.

Week 4: Walking with God

Day 1: The Acceptable Life (Mic. 6:6–8)

Micah asks three questions in Micah 6:6–8: (1) What brings us into God's presence (v. 6)? (2) What brings us into God's favor ("Will the LORD be pleased?" v. 7)? And (3) what brings us into God's peace (How do I deal with my sin? v. 7)? The answer is, not "going over the top" in the use of ritual (vv. 6–7)—that is, not going beyond what the Lord asks (v. 7) but just holding to "what is good" (v. 8). This involves the required sacrifices in the context of (1) living a just life ("do justice"), (2) having a true devotion ("love kindness," i.e., "maintain steadfast love" to God and man), and (3) keeping humble fellowship with God. In this threefold prescription we see how very personal was the religious life of the Old Testament—and is the religious life of the Bible.

Day 2: The Routine of True Religion (Deut. 16:16–17)

Elkanah went yearly to Shiloh (1 Sam. 1:3); Joseph and Mary went yearly to Jerusalem (Luke 2:41). This annual pilgrimage was costly in time, money, and effort. But the Lord's actual requirement was three times a year: (1) the Feast of Unleavened Bread (Deut. 16:1–8), the popular name for the Passover, when they came to remember their redemption; (2) the Feast of Weeks, at the start of the harvest season, later called Pentecost, a feast of joy because bondage in Egypt was past (vv. 9–12); and (3) the Feast of Booths, when the full harvest was home, remembering God's provision and care in the wilderness days (vv. 13–15). All three feasts were a special entrance into the Lord's presence (v. 16) and a chance to express devotion in proportionate giving (v. 17). No lukewarm religion this!

Day 3: Keeping in Touch (Dan. 6:1–10; Ps. 55:16–17)

Daniel's life was that of a top civil servant in a huge empire, but he made time for his personal prayer. He was threatened by jealousy but did not forsake the discipline and joy of three daily periods of quiet with God (Dan. 6:1–10). David's life was such that, given a chance, he would have grown wings and flown away. But though wings were impossible, flight was not, and he flew to God three times a day—as the day ended, as it began, and in the heart of its midday pressures (Ps. 55:16–17). How very slack we allow ourselves to be!

Day 4: The Wonder of Prayer and the Rest
It Brings (1 Sam. 1:4–17)

Elkanah did his good-humored best, but what Hannah needed was not "Am I not more to you than ten sons?" (1 Sam. 1:8) but "Dear Hannah, you are better to me than ten sons." And in addition to being childless, Hannah had to put up with Peninnah and her ceaseless teasing. So she took it to the Lord in prayer, and when she returned from the place of prayer, everything except one thing was still the same: she was still childless, Peninnah was still teasing, Elkanah was still his uncomprehending self, but her heart was no longer sad (v. 18). Prayer does change things.

Day 5: Telling God to His Face! (Jer. 12:1–5)

There is a blunt straightness about much Old Testament praying. The people knew the Lord well enough to vent their frustrations to him, rather than retiring hurt and chewing the fat to themselves. Jeremiah believed rightly that God is absolutely righteous (Jer. 12:1), but there was so much in the world that seemed downright unjust and unfair (vv. 1–2), for look how life treated Jeremiah, who served God with all his might (v. 3). Hannah (see day 4) took her sorrows to the Lord; Jeremiah took his problems with life to the Lord. Verse 5 is the Lord's reply: today's experiences are tomorrow's training ground. A good lesson to learn. And so is the lesson that we can explode to the Lord in our prayers.

Day 6: Times of Special Commitment (Num. 6:1–8)

A person became a Nazirite in order, for a fixed time, to show special devotion to the Lord (Num. 6:2). Alcohol (vv. 3–4) represented life's joys, and the Nazirite would now seek all his joys in the Lord. Hair (v. 5) represented the output of bodily strength, and all his vigor would now be for the Lord. Separation (v. 6) acknowledged the paramount claim of the Lord on time and relationships, even a family bereavement (v. 7). A Nazirite wanted to be holy, wholly for the Lord. It is easy to say, but should we not be like that in principle all the time? Of course, yes! But the Old Testament is so practical. Life offers many attractive joys within the will of God, many calls on time and strength of which he would approve, many dear personal bonds of love that he gladly allows us. It is good to set aside a fixed time solely for him.

Day 7: The People of the Book (Neh. 8:1–8)

Nehemiah 8 is one of the last pictures we have of the Lord's people in the Old Testament. They are gathered around the

Word of God, unanimous and eager to hear the Bible (v. 1), recognizing an obligation that all who can understand will give their absorbed attention (vv. 2–3), reverencing the Word (v. 5), and listening to those who can make its meaning clear (vv. 6–8). They know that this book was the product of human authorship (v. 1); nevertheless, it was the Lord's Word: designed by him as "Law," his own teaching for his people (v. 8). Such is the whole Bible to us.

OLD TESTAMENT WORSHIP

Meet the Congregations of the Church as They Brought Their Prayers and Praises to God

Week 1: Some Favorite Psalms: A Taste of a Wonderful Part of the Bible

Day 1: The Majestic Lord (Psalm 8)

Here is something typical of the Psalms: everything starts with God, not with the world around or with people. The Psalms are God-centered, and here is his greatness in relation to the earth and the heavens (Ps. 8:1), his greatness as Creator (v. 3) and as the One who orders life on earth (vv. 6–8), giving man and beast their respective places in the scheme of things. The "name" of the Lord (vv. 1, 9) is shorthand for all that he has revealed to be true about himself. "Majestic" puts him at the pinnacle of the power structure; as to "glory" (v. 1), his is higher than the highest we know; as to power (v. 3), his fingers are sufficient to position moon and stars. Yet he, literally, "remembers" and "visits" us (v. 4).

Day 2: The Shepherd and His Sheep (Psalm 23)

Every aspect of life comes in the brief six verses of Psalm 23: verse 2, rest and activity; verse 3, the inward soul and the outward path; verses 4–5, life's troubles and life's happiness; verse 5, hospitality and hostility; verses 5–6, present and future. And all this varied life is lived within the Shepherd's care, where the sheep is at rest and in safety. See how the *he* of verses 2 and 3 becomes the more directly personal *you* of verse 4, and how the Shepherd who leads ahead (v. 2) becomes the guardian alongside (v. 4)—for the deeper the darkness, the closer the presence. His protection surrounds us, as he goes before (v. 2), walks alongside (v. 4), and, in goodness and love, follows behind (v. 6). The chief virtue of a sheep is to relax, rest, and leave it to the Shepherd.

Day 3: Present Help (Psalm 46)

Psalm 46 is all *about* God, until suddenly (v. 10) he speaks for himself: "Relax . . . I am God." Circumstances (vv. 2–3) were hostile, waters roaring; people (v. 6) were hostile, nations roaring; but the Lord said, "Relax . . . I am God." As our "refuge" (v. 1), we can run to him; as "with us" (vv. 7, 11), he has come to us; as "strength" and "help" (v. 1), he is enough for each day's need; as "fortress" (vv. 7, 11, lit., "top security"), he lifts us out of the reach of threat. So, "Relax . . . I am God."

Day 4: To Be a Pilgrim (Psalm 84)

The Psalms reveal God's people enjoying his presence everywhere, yet there was one special place of his presence for Old Testament people, his "dwelling place" (Ps. 84:1), the Jerusalem temple. To be there was the great object of heart longing. To be there was a special blessing. In the birds flying and nesting in the temple the psalmist saw a parable: what a place of safety it was! Even though there was a constantly burning fire on the altar, a bird could safely nest, and so might each and all of his people find peace with God there. No wonder, then, that the pilgrimage (vv. 5–6), though demanding, was gladly endured. The envisaged benefits (vv. 10–12) more than compensated—the sunlight and shelter of his presence, and his grace and glory ("favor and honor") awaiting the pilgrim walker (v. 11).

Day 5: Worshiping and Listening (Psalm 95)

Psalm 95 is in three parts: (1) Verses 1–5 are an invitation followed by an explanation: we are called to worship because of what the Lord is—"great," the "great King," sovereign over every aspect of the world. (2) Verses 6–7a are an invitation followed by an explanation: we are called to worship because of what we are—his "people," his "sheep." (3) Verses 7b–11 show that the place of singing and bowing in worship is also the place of listening to the Lord's Word, so as to embark on a life of trust. Meribah and Massah were two names for a waterless place on the road from Egypt where the people grumbled in doubt rather than trusting in faith that the Lord would provide (see Exodus 17). He loves to be worshiped, heard, and trusted.

Day 6: The Father with a Mother's Love (Psalm 103)

This title for Psalm 103 expresses what verse 13 says: "Like as a father has a mother's love for his children" (my trans.)—"Like as a mother comforts her darling, answers his crying with a kind, loving tone, folds in her arms, and carries and soothes him, so the Lord loves and comforts his own." Look up Isaiah 49:15. But love cannot be seen as love until it does something for the loved one: how deeply do we prize the Lord's forgiveness (Ps. 103:3), redemption (v. 4), renewing strength (v. 5), his all-covering love (v. 11), his eternal love (v. 17)?

Day 7: Great . . . Gracious . . . Righteous (Psalm 145)

Psalm 145 is built around three words—"great," "gracious," "righteous"—in verses 3, 8, and 17, but what a wonderful collection of the attributes of God the whole psalm is. He is powerful (vv. 4–6, 12); tenderly good (vv. 7, 9); caring and provident (vv. 14–16); and (almost the most precious of all) "near" (v. 18), for the word contains the idea of the "next of kin"—the one who, in the Old Testament, freely shoulders our burdens, meets our needs, makes our wants his own. Rightly, the psalm is one of first-person singular response (vv. 1–2, 21).

Week 2: Psalms in the Life of David

Day 1: Getting on Top of Things
(Psalm 59; Background: 1 Sam. 19:9–17)

David was on the run from Saul's hit men. The story in 1 Samuel 19 only tells the beginning and end of the incident. Psalm 59 reveals the daily and nightly pressure under which David lived. How did he rise above it? (1) He prayed (vv. 1–5): the first move in times of pressure is to "take it to the Lord in prayer." (2) He trusted (vv. 9–10), watching not for his enemies to attack but for God to come to his aid. (3) He found security in God: in verses 1, 9, 16, and 17, "protect" and "fortress" express the idea of "top security," a lifting up (inaccessibly) above the threat. How surprised the watching hit men must have been to hear David and Michal singing and making music to God while still in the thick of their trouble (vv. 16–17).

Day 2: Where the Real Shelter Is
(Psalm 57; Background: 1 Samuel 22:1)

Humanly speaking, how cornered David must have felt—a fugitive from Saul, sneaking into a cave for shelter (Psalm 57 title): the cold stone of the rock around and overhead, the menacing beasts outside (v. 4). But bring together the words in the title, "in the cave," and the words in verse 1, "in the shadow of your wings." As David looked at the overshadowing cave walls, it was not stone he saw but the sheltering, comforting wings of his God, brooding over and around him like a great mother bird. Isn't this a real "practicing of the presence of God"—not in the sense of trying to force ourselves to feel he is with us but in the deeper sense of resting on his promise that he will never leave us (Heb. 13:5–6)?

Day 3: The Power of Repentance
(Ps. 51:1–6; Background: 2 Samuel 11–12)

The most important word in Psalm 51:1–6 is "for," at the beginning of verse 3. It explains how all the benefits of verses 1 and 2 can be experienced. In David there is "transgression, iniquity, sin," but in the Lord there is "mercy, love, compassion," whereby sin can be "blotted out, washed away, cleansed" (NIV). But the clue to the experience of forgiveness is acknowledging that I am a sinner—just that (vv. 3–4). David does not specify his particular sins of adultery and murder at this time, because what he says is true of all sins. It could not be put better than 2 Samuel 12:13.

Day 4: The Prayer of the Penitent (Ps. 51:7–19)

David's prayer in Psalm 51 touches on four topics and becomes a model prayer for us as we too repent before God: (1) to be accepted before God (vv. 7–9)—our sins offend him and need to be blotted out; (2) to be rid of sin (vv. 10–12)—true repentance must be accompanied by a real desire to become a different person; (3) to tell others about this praiseworthy God (vv. 13–15); and (4) to ask God to put right all the harm our sin has done to others (vv. 16–19). David was king and knew rightly that his sin was destructive for his kingdom. But the same is true of us in the body of Christ. We never sin, however privately, without hurting the body.

Day 5: Peace in Time of Stress
(Psalm 3; Background: 2 Samuel 15–17)

When his eldest surviving son rebelled against him, David made a strategic withdrawal eastward from Jerusalem, over the Kidron and the northern slopes of Olives to Bahurim, then across Jordan and north thirty miles to Mahanaim. Psalm 3 is the product of the first night on that weary road, when God visited him with a surprising peace and a good night's sleep (vv. 5–6). How did such calm come to him? (1) By seeing that God is sufficient even for this emergency (vv. 1–3), and (2) by discovering that prayer brings peace and real assurance about the future (vv. 4–8). First he turns to God, and then, in answer to prayer, he receives from God an experience of rest (Phil. 4:6–7), and finally he goes forward with God into the threatening future.

Day 6: Thirsty—but for God
(Psalm 63; Background: 2 Samuel 15–17)

On the second night of the flight from Absalom, sleep eludes David (Ps. 63:6). Yet his thoughts (marvelously) are not self-pitying; rather, the wearying, waterless terrain through which he has marched that day becomes a picture of a dry soul longing for God (v. 1). This longing finds expression in remembering and praising (vv. 2–6), joy in divine help (vv. 7–8), trust for the future (vv. 9–11). Note the spirit of determination all the way through: "I seek" (v. 1); "I will bless" (v. 4); "my mouth will praise" (v. 5); "I remember . . . meditate" (v. 6); "I will sing" (v. 7); "my soul clings to you" (v. 8, lit., "my soul follows you closely").

Day 7: Out of the Depths
(Psalm 30; Background: 2 Sam. 5:6–13)

If the "house" (not "temple," as ESV) in the heading of Psalm 30 is David's own house, then we learn that as he planned to "move in," he was visited by a potentially terminal illness (vv. 6–10). Certainly the passage in 2 Samuel breathes a complacently confident spirit that the world was now at David's feet. The perils of a day of prosperity are greater than those of a day of difficulty. He needed the shock realization of his fragility to bring him to his spiritual senses—his total dependence in prayer (vv. 1–3), a true understanding of his experience (vv. 6–7)—with resultant joy and thanksgiving (vv. 11–12).

Week 3: Facing Life

Day 1: The Key to All Life (Psalm 1)

(1) *Commitment* (Ps. 1:1): alter the translation to "has determined not to walk . . . stand . . . sit." (2) *Contrast* (v. 2): a very different foundation for life—not the "counsel of the wicked" but the "law" (i.e., "teaching") of the Lord, capturing our hearts ("delights") and our minds ("meditates"). (3) *Consequence* (v. 3): the Hebrew suggests "and consequently he is like . . ."; "planted" is literally "transplanted." Dwelling on God's Word brings us into a new position where life is refreshed by streams of water and bears fruit. After "prospers" (v. 3), imagine the words "in the Lord's time," for the psalmist is too wise to think that prosperity is automatic! (4) *Condemnation* (vv. 4–5). (5) *Confidence* (v. 6): ever in his care.

Day 2: Facing Adversity (Ps. 37:1–11)

There is nothing out of date about the problem of seeing people who never think of God prospering and reaching positions of influence, while those who are devoted to him are busy getting nowhere, seeing none of their hopes fulfilled (Ps. 37:4), possibly under a cloud of false accusation (v. 6)—no sign of the meek inheriting the earth (v. 11). In this life things are all too often far from ideal, very unfair, and unjust too. The reply of Psalm 37 sounds simplistic but is simply effective. It is the life of trust and commitment, patience, personal restraint, and trustful expectation. In short, the God-centered life.

Day 3: Depression (Psalm 42)

Talking to oneself, they say, is the first sign of madness. Maybe. But giving oneself a good talking to is one of the signs of spiritual health. This is exactly what Psalm 42 is doing. Since the psalmist is fondly recalling temple festivals (v. 4) but now hears the thunder of waterfalls in Hermon (vv. 6–7) and is surrounded by mockers (vv. 3, 10), we must imagine an exile from his Jerusalem home—tearful (v. 3), oppressed (v. 7), and suffering (v. 10). What a recipe for depression. He *is* downcast (vv. 5, 11), but he is not lying down under it, grumbling, self-pitying, "chewing the fat." He is directive with himself, determined to bring God into his life (v. 6), and frank with God about his problems (v. 7). Above all, he maintains a sure hope (vv. 5, 11).

Day 4: Earthly Inequalities, Heavenly Benefits (Psalm 49)

He is a confident chap, this psalmist. There is a problem in Psalm 49, but he has a solution (vv. 1–4). The problem is "wicked deceivers" (v. 5 NIV) who are doing very nicely, thank you (vv. 16, 18). So had he, or a friend, just lost out to a crooked finance company? That's the sort of situation in any case. What, then, is the solution to facing a life that contains all too much of this kind of thing? Think about death and the life to come. *They* have no hopeful expectation in death (vv. 13–14); for us, on the contrary, after death, all present inequalities will be corrected (v. 14), and redemption awaits (v. 15), not as captives of the grave but as those "taken" by the Lord to himself (cf. Gen. 5:24).

Day 5: God Is My Portion (Psalm 73)

Psalm 73 continues the thought of Psalm 49. Faith says how good God is, but life often seems to contradict this (73:1–3). Those who are spiritually careless prosper, while the devoted person has trouble on trouble (vv. 4–14). But wait. Think in terms of eternal destiny (v. 17). The contrast between verses 18–20 and 23–25 could not be more complete. What richness is here—to experience God's presence and his holding hand, his plan over all our life and experiences, and "afterward . . . glory" (v. 24). It is only those who are sure about heaven who have the strength and insight to manage life on earth.

Day 6: The Lifeline of Prayer (Psalm 107:1–22)

Psalm 107 is as good a collection of the different experiences of God's people as we will easily find. The first "some" (vv. 4–5) experienced privation and hostile circumstances; the second "some" (vv. 10–11) brought themselves into bondage by flouting God's will; the third "some" (vv. 17–18) made their lives miserable by rebellious, unruly ways. But they all had this in common: they met life's difficulties head-on in prayer (vv. 6, 13, 19) and experienced the Lord's sufficient answers (vv. 7, 14, 20). Psalm 65:2 has a lovely title for the Lord: "O you who hear prayer."

Day 7: No Escape . . . No Regrets (Psalm 139)

Psalm 139:7–12 reviews a variety of possible "escapes" from God, not because the psalmist wants to get away from him but because he needs the comfort of reminding himself that he cannot. He wrote in a time of distress: there were people around him whose only desire was to speak ill of the Lord (vv. 19–22). The strength of his reaction to them reveals the depth of his horror at what they represented and of the hurt they gave him. But in this shadow hanging over his life he had a secure refuge in God, from whom there was no escape: this wonderful God knew all about him (vv. 1–4), hemmed him in, not restrictively but protectively, and sheltered him with his own hand (v. 5). God was present with him in every place (vv. 7–12). From such a safe place in God, life can be faced.

Week 4: The Individual and the World: Two Prominent Themes in the Psalms

Day 1: Time of Trouble, Time of . . . ? (Ps. 119:25–32)

"I," "me," "my" come in every line of this reading from Psalm 119, typical of the very personal religion of the Psalms; typically too, the individual is in trouble. How do we react to a time of trouble? The writer of this psalm reacted (1) by making it a time of prayer—seven of the eight verses in this section are prayers, more than in any other part of Psalm 119; (2) by recognizing it as a time of temptation (vv. 28–29), a special request to be kept from taking false paths; and (3) by making it a time of commitment—to meditate on God's Word, choose his way, hold fast, and make a special effort (vv. 27, 30–32).

Day 2: Light and Salvation (Psalm 27)

Again, "I," "me," "my" come in every verse in Psalm 27 (except v. 14, which is probably David giving an order to himself). It says, (1) my security is in the Lord (vv. 1–3); (2) my longing is for the Lord (vv. 4–6); (3) my confidence is in the Lord, whose devotion to me is more certain than (even) parental love (vv. 7–10); and (4) my future rests with the Lord, who will lead, protect, and bring me through (vv. 11–13). Therefore (v. 14) he takes himself in hand and tells himself what to do (see week 3, day 3).

Day 3: Sixfold Keeping (Psalm 121)

The verb "keep" occurs six times in Psalm 121 (vv. 3, 4, 5, 7 [2x], 8)—a psalm of our sixfold security in the Lord's care. Whatever the threat was—maybe we are not told in order that we can slot our own problem in—the psalm says that the answer lies in the great Creator God who keeps each of his people and all his people (vv. 1–4). He keeps us sheltered from real dangers (like sunstroke) and imaginary ones (like moonstroke), in a round-the-clock vigil (vv. 5–6). He keeps us from all harm for all time, beginning now (vv. 7–8). Verse 3 shows how detailed his care is; verse 5, how personal, interposing himself between us and the threat; and verses 7–8, how total.

Day 4: Personal Prayer, Personal Commitment (Ps. 116:1–14)

Psalm 116 too originated in a time of trouble that became the occasion of prayer (vv. 3–4). This is not as easy as it sounds. In our experience the time of trouble is so often the time when it is hardest to pray, even though, by failing to pray, we cut ourselves off from our surest comfort and help. The experience of answered prayer led the psalmist to a deeper love for the Lord (vv. 1–2), a clearer knowledge of God's gracious character (vv. 5–6), and a definite personal commitment to respond to the Lord in daily life (vv. 9, 12). The order of verses 13 and 14 is important. Always, our first response is to take what the Lord freely gives; only then can we take up the task of living out the godly life in the fellowship of his people.

Day 5: King of Zion . . . King of the World (Psalm 2)

The Psalms have a clear vision for the world—of a great, divine King reigning over the whole world from Zion. The Lord promised David a continuing line of kings (2 Sam. 7:16), but at some point this developed into the expectation of a special son of David who would also be the Son of God and who would reign forever. Think, then, of Psalm 2 as a coronation song, composed for the day when one of the Davidic kings ascended the throne. Would he be the promised Messiah? The vision of the ideal is held up before him: this is what he should be—the "son" (v. 7), the world's king (v. 8), and the one in whom any and all can find refuge (v. 12). We are privileged to belong to that Zion (Heb. 12:22–24) and to live under that King (Luke 1:30–33).

Day 6: When the Lord Comes to Reign (Psalm 96)

Parallel with the expectation of the perfect King was the expectation that it would be the Lord himself who would come to reign. Already his people know him as the great King (Ps. 95:3; 96:4) and have the duty to make him known worldwide (v. 10). But when he does come to reign, all creation will be "set to rights" (vv. 11–13)—a good translation of "judge" in verse 13. God the Creator will not desert his creation or allow the damage and corruption brought by sin (Gen. 3:18) to have the last word. He will come. He will reign. And there will be a new heaven and a new earth (Isa. 11:6–9; 65:17–25; Rev. 21:1–5).

Day 7: The Lord's Worldwide People (Psalm 100)

"From earth's wide bounds, from ocean's farthest coast, through gates of pearl streams in the countless host, singing to Father, Son, and Holy Ghost: Hallelujah."[1] The hymn finds its fulfillment in Revelation 7:9–10 but its inspiration in Psalm 100. This lovely psalm is a threefold call twice repeated (vv. 1–2, "Make a joyful noise . . . serve . . . come"; verse 4, "Enter . . . give thanks . . . bless"), followed each time by an explanation (v. 3, "the LORD, he is God"; v. 5, "the LORD is good"). Because he is God, we are safe in his care (v. 3); because he is good, we experience his unchanging, faithful love (v. 5).

OLD TESTAMENT PROPHECY
Meet and Hear the Great Preachers

Week 1: Meet the Prophets

Day 1: The Voice of God through a Broken Heart (Hos. 1:1–8; 3:1–2)

Hosea ministered in the northern kingdom, Israel, at a time of great material prosperity but steep decline in true religion and spirituality. The Lord spoke to him through a bitter sadness in his own home: the infidelity of his wife—so we gather from hints dropped. It is only of his first child that it says she "bore him" (Hos. 1:3), and by 3:2 he has to buy her, presumably as one would a prostitute. Hosea 3:1 is the verse to concentrate on. Hosea's love for Gomer is modeled on the Lord's love for his people, an undying love for us in our waywardness, love that reaches out to seek and to save and to bring home.

---

1. William Walsham How, Anglican Bishop of Wakefield, "For All the Saints" (1864).

Day 2: Resolute Prophet . . . Unstoppable Word (Amos 7:10–17)

A little before Hosea (about 750 BC), Amos too prophesied to Israel. He got into trouble with "the establishment" through denouncing the pursuit of affluence at the expense of the poor and of spiritual values. Amos was confident of the call of God (Amos 7:14–15); he knew that what he was saying was what the Lord says (v. 17) and that no opposition could stop the word (vv. 16–17). All the prophets were the same. And in our situation, if we are to "go public for God," we need to be as confident as Amos that we are following his call and that we possess, and are determined to share, the unstoppable Word of God, the Bible.

Day 3: Wrestling, Waiting, Trusting (Hab. 2:1–4; 3:17–19)

The prophets were truly human. The confidence with which they proclaimed the word of God when they received it was often the end product of wrestling to understand just what God was doing and planning. Habakkuk had two problems with this that we can identify: Why does God seem to do nothing about the wickedness in the world (Hab. 1:2)? And why, when he acts, does he use such unworthy agents—in this case the Babylonians (1:5–6, 13)? The answer the Lord gave him and his response to it will do for us too: hold to what the Lord has spoken (2:2), wait for his word to be fulfilled (2:3), and trust him come what may (2:4; 3:17–19).

Day 4: Second Chance (Jonah 1:1–3; 3:1–3)

What a very human prophet was Jonah! Unlike Isaiah with his prompt "Send me" (Isa. 6:8), Jonah rather replied, "What! Me?" and quickly set off in the opposite direction. Did the Lord then give up on Jonah and look for someone else? Certainly not! He does not give us up; he pursues us to bring us back into his will; he gives a second chance (Jonah 3:1). Somehow, in God's way of doing things, only Jonah will do as a prophet to Nineveh. This is the serious importance of the individual in the plan of God. There is no such thing as "Here I am, send him or her." Each holds a key place that no one else can fill.

Day 5: Not an Afterthought (Jer. 1:4–9)

Jeremiah did not run away, but like Jonah, he did say, "What! Me?" (Jer. 1:6), through a sense of inability ("I do not know how") and immaturity ("only a youth"). The Lord met him with three assurances: (1) he had long since prepared Jeremiah for all this (v. 5; cf. Eph. 1:4; 2:10); (2) he would keep Jeremiah company all through the hard slog of obedience (Jer. 1:8); and (3) he gave him the words to say (v. 9), with the assurance that he would make his word effective (v. 12). Jeremiah's book shows that the prophet never did stop trembling, nor lose his sense of inadequacy. But neither did he let his feelings prevent him from obeying.

Day 6: The Great God of the Prophets (Ezek. 1:1–3, 28; 2:1–4)

The "thirtieth year" (Ezek. 1:1) may be Ezekiel's age—the time when, as a priest (v. 3), he would in other circumstances have begun his priestly service. But he was a captive exile in Babylon. On this day of disappointed hopes he was granted "visions of God" (v. 1) and a sense of the hand of God on his life (v. 3). The Lord is never defeated by our circumstances or our disappointments. Furthermore, the vision was one of surrounding divine mercy and care, for the rainbow is the sign of God's protective promises (v. 28; Gen. 9:13–16). Great as was the God whom Ezekiel saw in visions, he intended that this man should come into his fellowship and hear his word (Ezek. 2:1–2). The prophets were unique, but for us too God is caring, undefeated, opening his fellowship, sharing his Word.

Day 7: Speaking for God in the Day of Inflation (Hag. 1:1–7)

The exile was over and the people back from Babylon. It was a time of prosperity and comfort, living in "paneled houses" (Hag. 1:4), the equivalent of cavity-wall insulation—pretty luxurious. But for all their expenditure on self, it was hard to make ends meet. The economy was depressed, they weren't really satisfied, and the money seemed to go nowhere (v. 6). But without a house, how could the Lord come to live among them? That's what the house meant. They thought they could manage just as well without his indwelling presence.

Week 2: The Prophets' Word and Message

Day 1: The Actual Words of God (Ezek. 2:7–3:4)

What the Lord asked was surely impossible—to "speak my words" (Ezek. 2:7)? Note the plural—not just the general idea of what the Lord wanted to be said but the actual words. This could happen only through the miracle of inspiration, and it was "pictured" to Ezekiel as being given a book to eat. He took into himself the words God had written, and when he had received them, he was able to obey and "speak with my words" (3:4). In all this Ezekiel remained a real person, called to make his own commitment and to obey God's Word himself (2:8). The miracle of inspiration did not override or overrule his personality. As preacher of the Word, he had to be the first to obey it.

Day 2: A Careful Record (Jer. 36:1–5, 17–18)

What a vivid picture. The Lord spoke (Jer. 36:2–3), Jeremiah dictated, and Baruch wrote it all down (vv. 4, 18). The book was at one and the same time God's words, Jeremiah's words, and Baruch's words. Each had his place. The Lord reveals what he wants to say; Jeremiah is inspired to receive and transmit it; and Baruch makes an exact record, word by word. This insight into the way one prophet safeguarded his message is true of the whole Bible: the word of God, the word of the human author, the word of the careful scribe.

Day 3: Focus on God (Isa. 30:8–11)

A "tablet" (Isa. 30:8) is what we would call a "billboard." The Chinese "wall newspaper" is, perhaps, a modern equivalent. This was how Isaiah made his message available to a wider public. But there is something else here too: we often think of the prophets as if they were primarily social reformers, challenging injustice and inequality. But actually, first and foremost, they spoke about God. This was what Isaiah's people found uncomfortable and unacceptable—"let us hear no more about the Holy One" (v. 11).

Day 4: A Worldview: Crimes against Humanity (Amos 1:13–2:3)

The prophets were social commentators too. Here we find Amos reviewing the crimes of the surrounding nations: (1) Ammon the imperialist, whose only concern was to "extend his borders" and who allowed no concern for human helplessness (the pregnant woman and the unborn child) to stand in the way (Amos 1:13); and (2) Moab the vengeful, who reached back into the past to exact retribution on a corpse (2:1). The Ammonite Wars are known in history; the act of Moab is known only in Amos. But all crimes against people are known in heaven and will unfailingly be judged and punished. A solemn and salutary thought for the savage world in which we live.

Day 5: Religion without Morality? (Jer. 7:1–11)

The Jerusalem temple was the "house" in which the Lord lived among his people. Because they had the temple, they thought they had God too and must therefore be safe whatever danger threatened. To Jeremiah, a religion without moral commitment is a deception (Jer. 7:4). This is what he meant by the accusation that they were treating the house as robbers treat their den (v. 11)—a place of safety without thought of moral reformation. To Jeremiah (and all the prophets and all the Bible), a religion that failed to change lives was meaningless (James 1:26–27).

Day 6: Talking Pictures (Zech. 2:1–5)

After the exile, Zechariah did what prophets often did: used pictures to tell the truth. In his time Jerusalem was still in ruins.

There would have been much discussion about rebuilding plans and what the cost would be. The picture of stopping the surveyor from measuring the dimensions of old Jerusalem was a vivid way of saying that the Lord is not limited to the past. With him we should always have larger, grander visions of what he will do in the future. This is a real message for us, whether we think of our church or of our own lives: with God the best is always yet to be.

Day 7: The Glorious Future (Mic. 4:1–5)

What a marvelous prospect—a world united around the Lord, magnetized by his truth, living at peace under his rule, without need either of weapons or of military training. This is what Jerusalem on its hill was always meant to be: a magnet to the world, holding the truth in order to share the truth (Mic. 4:2). While the New Testament stresses "going out" to share the truth, it also agrees with the Old Testament that the Lord's people should be magnets: the quality of our individual and corporate lives "attracting" those who are still outside. This is the point of Micah's determination to "walk in the name of the LORD" (v. 5)—to live for him the life that speaks to others and draws them in.

Week 3: Amos, a Typical Prophet: Disaster and Hope

Day 1: The Cardinal Sin of the Lord's People (Amos 2:4–12)

The formula "three . . . four" (Amos 2:1) is as if to say, "Three sins would be enough, but the fourth—that's the last straw!" Up to the point of today's reading, Amos has been addressing pagan nations (see week 2, day 4), but now he turns to the Lord's people in their two sections, Judah (vv. 4–5) and Israel (vv. 6–12), and finally both together (3:1–8). What does the Lord find to be the "last straw" in the case of his people? To reject his "law" (i.e., "teaching," 2:4) and to silence the voice of his prophets (vv. 11–12). Of course, their social and religious misconduct matters (vv. 6–8). What matters most of all, however, is that God taught them his truth, and they would not learn; he spoke to them by his prophets, and they would not listen. To possess the Word of God is to be judged by our use of this privilege.

Day 2: A Word to Be Trusted (Amos 3:1–8)

Amos 3:1–8 focuses on two things: (1) the unique relationship between the Lord and his people (v. 2), and (2) the significance of the voice of the prophet (vv. 3–8). In this way Amos is continuing the teaching from yesterday's reading about the people of God possessing the Word of God. Privilege brings peril (vv. 1–2): the more God entrusts to us, the more searching will be his inquiry into our response to our privileges; God's Word cannot fail to be effective (vv. 3–8). The seven pictures in verses 3–6 illustrate cause and effect. But there is a final cause that should bring about its proper effect: when the Lord speaks his Word, it is like the roar of a great lion, and there should be a prompt response.

Day 3: Prepare to Meet God (Amos 4:4–13)

As Amos saw, the people were extraordinarily religious—and even punctilious over it. Yet he recognized all this as simply another way of sinning and of being self-pleasing (Amos 4:4–5). Meanwhile, through their circumstances—famine, drought, blight, plague, war, and calamity on a grand scale—the Lord was laboring to achieve what *he* wanted to see in them: a true repentance and return to God, a personal relationship in which sin was acknowledged and God sought (vv. 6–11). If Jeremiah's people wanted religion without morality (see week 2, day 5), Amos's people wanted religion without the personal dimension of repentance—reconciliation with God and a closeness of relationship with him, literally, a "coming right up to me."

Day 4: The Penalty of Complacency (Amos 6:1–7)

In the society around him Amos saw unconcern regarding divine judgment (Amos 6:3, "the day of disaster"), oppressive rule (v. 3, "violence"), self-indulgent lifestyle (v. 4, "beds . . . couches . . .

lambs"), and lavish expenditure on luxury (v. 6, "wine in bowls . . . finest oils"). All this was bracketed by a complacent sense of their own security and a total unconcern about national welfare (vv. 1–6). (Maybe "Joseph" [v. 6] symbolizes those who could be hurt and dominated by more powerful interests, like Joseph in his brothers' power: heedlessness about the vulnerable members of society.) For such people Amos saw no hope.

Day 5: Hope and No Hope (Amos 7:1–9)

In Amos 7 two acts of divine judgment are prayed against (locusts and fire, vv. 1–3, 4–6), and in allowing that prayer, the Lord is setting his face against any and every judgment that would totally destroy his people. But one judgment on them is neither prayed against nor averted—the plumb line (vv. 7–9). The wall was "built with a plumb line" (v. 7) and, when built, would be tested by the same plumb line. At the very beginning the Lord gave Moses a plumb line for building up the life of his people: the *law of God* as the standard for their conduct and the *grace of God* (expressed in the atoning sacrifices) by which their lapses from obedience would be covered and forgiven. It was by this double standard that they would be judged: did they commit themselves to obey? Did they run to God for forgiveness when they failed to obey (1 John 1:7)?

Day 6: Market Forces (Amos 8:1–8)

What a vision of sweeping judgment (Amos 8:3, 8)! What could have caused such rage?

1. Exploitation in society (v. 4), especially of the "poor" and "needy," whose poverty made them easy game and readily exploitable
2. An overriding interest in moneymaking (v. 5) and resentment if religion kept the shop closed
3. Commercial dishonesty (v. 5), selling under weight and overcharging for it

4. Using money and goods in bribery and corruption (v. 6)
5. Making a profit out of inferior goods (v. 6)

All this, the Lord said, he would never forget (v. 7). This is the authentic voice of the prophet's social conscience.

Day 7: The Sieve of the Lord (Amos 9:9–15)

We saw (day 5) how the Lord turned away from judgments that would destroy his people. Here is the glorious other side of the same divine purpose: he will sieve out his people (Amos 9:9), removing every complacent sinner (those who deny all adverse consequence of their sin, v. 10), and will bring in the perfect kingdom of David, worldwide, with abundant prosperity, restoring his people to their proper possessions and security of tenure (vv. 11–15).

Week 4: The Greatest Hope of All:
The Prophets and the Coming Messiah

Day 1: The Baby Who Is God and King (Isa. 9:1–7)

Isaiah lived through the dreadful Assyrian invasions (711–705 BC) and saw the northern areas fall to the conqueror (Isa. 9:1). Looking forward he also saw that where darkness first fell, light would first dawn (v. 2): a remarkable prediction in that Jesus spent his early life and his first ministry in Galilee. Isaiah saw the coming day as one of joy, victory, and liberation (vv. 3–4)—all because a baby was born, God himself come to birth, the bringer of peace, the inheritor of David's throne, and the promised worldwide ruler (vv. 6–7).

Day 2: Glad Hope for All Nations (Isa. 25:1–9)

The prophets, looking forward, saw all the world caught up into God's blessing. Isaiah 25 is in fact the song sung by the worldwide pilgrims as they throng home into the city of God. They come singing of deliverance (vv. 1–5) and sit down to the great feast

(vv. 6–9) where every need is supplied, every shadow dispelled (including the shadow of death), every sorrow banished, and all that people ever expected from God fulfilled, the days of waiting amply rewarded.

Day 3: The Great Shepherd of the Sheep (Ezek. 34:22–31)

Kings were often depicted as shepherds, the carers of their people. When the David-to-be was foreseen, the model of the perfect Shepherd lay ready at hand, as portrayed in Ezekiel 34. The picture corresponds to the past, present, and future of the Christian—the saving work of the "good shepherd" (John 10:14), the present care of the "Shepherd and Overseer of your souls" (1 Pet. 2:25), and the expectation of the coming "chief Shepherd" (1 Pet. 5:4).

Day 4: The Servant Messiah: His Birth and Work (Isa. 53:1–6)

"The arm of the LORD" (Isa. 53:1) is shorthand for "the Lord himself with his sleeves rolled up for action" (cf. 51:9–10; 52:10). Isaiah thus foresees God himself coming and growing up as a man among men (53:2–3). In verse 5, "for" means "because of." Ours was the transgression, his the suffering, the purpose of which was to bring us peace with God. Trace in verse 6 what is true of *all*, what is true of *each*, and what *the Lord* did about it. We can only marvel at the inspiration granted to Isaiah to foresee so minutely what would be fulfilled in the Lord Jesus.

Day 5: The Servant Messiah: His Death and Life (Isa. 53:7–12)

Isaiah follows the course of the Messiah's arrest (he could have resisted but chose not to, Isa. 53:7), the injustice of the procedure, and his vicarious suffering (v. 8). The mysterious reference to the "wicked" and the "rich" in burial (v. 9) remained unexplained until it happened (Matt. 27:38, 57). In all this the Servant-Messiah was guiltless (Isa. 53:9). Then comes the surprise: after all that bruising death, the Messiah is alive—"he shall prolong his days"—and active as the executor of the will of God (v. 10). Isaiah does not use the word "resurrection," but he shows the Servant vigorously and actively alive after death and burial. Verse 12 sums up his greatness (more accurately translated): "Therefore I will give him the many as his portion, and he will take the strong as his spoil."

Day 6: He Is Our Peace (Mic. 5:1–5a)

Micah 5 is another passage familiar in Christmas readings, and rightly so. David provided the model for much Old Testament expectation of the Messiah (see days 1 and 3)—the best of the past foreshadowing the perfection of the future. Even David's town was to be the birthplace of the coming King. Yet the vision was not of a mere David "look-alike." The Old Testament does not give all the answers but offers enigmas awaiting the fulfilled reality to explain them. So he will be born in Bethlehem, but his origins are "from ancient days" (v. 2). Only the incarnation fits the picture and explains what Micah was grasping after. But he leaves unexplained how the coming ruler will himself be our "peace" (v. 5). This has to await Ephesians 2:14–17.

Day 7: The Transforming Comforter (Isa. 61:1–3)

Isaiah completes his messianic preview (the King, day 1; the Servant, days 4 and 5) with the vision of the Anointed One (Isa. 61:1–3). This was the passage the Lord Jesus took as the text of his first recorded sermon (Luke 4:16–19). Significantly, he stopped reading at Isa. 61:2a, for his first coming was the year of favor, and the "day of vengeance" awaits his still-expected second coming (see 2 Thess. 1:7–9). The good news here (Isa. 61:1) is of his transforming power, touching and changing our sorrows, bondages, and bereavements.

OLD TESTAMENT WISDOM
Listen to the Voice of Wisdom
Discussing Life and Directing Conduct

Week 1: Proverbs—the Way of Wisdom

Day 1: Decisiveness (Prov. 1:8–19)

In the Bible, truth is not truly known until it changes the way we live. Instruction and teaching lead to outward beauty of life (Prov. 1:8–9). But such a life never goes unchallenged, and Proverbs now describes a young person facing a typical temptation to veer from the wise path (vv. 10–19)—to exploit other people for the sake of self-gain and to "keep in with your mates." But such a life offends God: it is sin, and sin always boomerangs (vv. 18–19). Characteristically, Proverbs begins by calling us to side decisively with the way of wisdom.

Day 2: Urgency (Prov. 1:20–33)

The message of Proverbs 1:20–33 is simple: the voice of wisdom is readily available, but if it is ignored, the day will come when our cry for wisdom will be ignored and we will get what we have chosen. Life is like that, so we should give close attention to the voice of God teaching us in the Word of God. This saves us from living without guiding principles, from cynically mocking true values, and from becoming moral fatheads.

Day 3: Getting Down to It (Prov. 2:1–11)

Notice the balance between "then" and "for" in Proverbs 2:5–6 and 9–10. When we work hard at wisdom, then understanding comes (v. 5), for it is in this way that the Lord gives wisdom (vv. 6–8). When he gives wisdom, then we understand how to live (v. 9), for wisdom grips our hearts and becomes a protective force in our lives (vv. 10–11). The conditions on which we may enjoy these benefits are open-minded acceptance of the Word of God, memorization (v. 1), attentiveness and mental application (v. 2), prayer (v. 3), and committed searching for the truth in its intrinsic value (v. 4).

Day 4: The Lord First (Prov. 3:1–13)

Life is a mix of good times and bad, prosperity and adversity. Over it all is the Lord, who makes things plain (Prov. 1:6) and prosperous (vv. 9–10) and who also disciplines and rebukes (vv. 11–12). Since all life is thus straight from the Lord's hand, our primary concern is not health and fitness programs (v. 8) or market forces (v. 10) but trusting (v. 5) and honoring him (v. 9) and bowing to his will with glad submissiveness (vv. 11–12).

Day 5: Personal Purity (Prov. 5:1–20)

When you read right through Proverbs, you will find that the theme of sexual purity and married joy in chapter 5 is recurrent throughout and that it is basic to the wise life. Proverbs hides nothing: sexual misbehavior, for all its promised sweetness, brings death (vv. 3–5), broken health (v. 11), belated self-awareness, and public disgrace (vv. 12–14). How fulfilling and entrancing by contrast is God's plan of marriage (vv. 15–19). And not only in sex but over the whole arena of life. The "why" of verse 20 challenges us to recognize that holiness wins every time over sin.

Day 6: Wisdom in Person (Prov. 8:12–31)

Whether we understand that wisdom is revealed in Proverbs 8 as a distinct divine person within the Godhead or that it is a dramatic personification of a divine attribute, the passage prepares us for the revelation of the Lord Jesus as the wisdom of God (1 Cor. 1:24, 30; 2:6–7; Col. 2:3). As we read, we can turn every thought into worship and praise of him in whom true wisdom is seen (Prov. 8:12–14), who is King of kings (vv. 15–16), in whom we find wisdom and its rewards (vv. 17–21)—the eternal One (vv. 22–26), present in the work of creation (vv. 27–31), and delighting in the divine handiwork (v. 31).

Day 7: Decisions, Decisions! (Prov. 9:1–18)

The first nine chapters of Proverbs are a unity in a way that is not true of the rest of the book. Note, therefore, how we return today in Proverbs 9 to the thoughts of the first two days: in this life alternative voices call to us (vv. 1, 13). The one has food in abundance and is hers to give (vv. 4–5); the other invites to a stolen banquet (v. 17). The one calls to life (v. 6); the other opens the door to death (v. 18). In one case, lack of guiding principle ("simple," v. 6) is transformed into wisdom and learning (v. 9); in the other, those who lack guiding principles (v. 16) are conducted to their death (v. 18). The choice is ours.

Week 2: Proverbs—Directives for the Wise

Day 1: Types and Talk (Prov. 10:22–32)

The fool (Prov. 10:23) is not so much the person who does not stop to think, as the one who has not got the clues or the abilities to think straight, the thickhead. By contrast, the wise learn from the wisdom of God. It is not accidental that Proverbs moves directly to the contrast between the righteous and the wicked (vv. 24, 28–30, 32). One thing leads to another. Typically, in Proverbs people are known by the way they talk (vv. 31–32). Sins of speech are in Proverbs' top three.

Day 2: Righteousness (Prov. 12:28–13:9)

Righteousness gives, guards, and promotes life (Prov. 12:28; 13:6, 9); wickedness brings overthrow and death (vv. 6, 9). This is the main thrust of this group of sayings and constitutes a call to moral commitment (v. 5). But the sayings about listening and talking (vv. 1–3) need to be pondered, as do the sharp observations that life must not be judged by appearance (v. 7) and that no one bothers to kidnap a poor man (v. 8). It is this mix of deep instruction, warning, and streetwise comment that makes Proverbs so rich.

Day 3: Living for the Lord (Prov. 15:33–16:7)

Proverbs 15:33–16:7 is a unique passage in Proverbs in that eight verses in turn mention the Lord. He is the Sovereign who has the last word in all our plans (16:1) and governs everything for his own purposes (v. 4); the fear of the Lord (the loving, careful reverence of 1 Pet. 1:17) directs (Prov. 15:33) and restrains (16:6); he knows and appraises our hearts (vv. 2, 5); he is active for those who live so as to please him (v. 7); and the truly successful life comes when we commit, or "roll onto," the Lord—like a burden we are glad to be rid of—all our work and all our plans (v. 3).

Day 4: Putting Your Heart into It (Prov. 23:12–19)

In the sayings in Proverbs 23:12–19, the heart is given characteristic prominence. It matters what things preoccupy our hearts (v. 12) and also the ambitions and aspirations we cherish there (v. 19), the desires to which we give heart room. The heart is ours to control, shutting out envy (lit., "covet"), insisting rather that it should be zealous for (better, "covet") reverence (v. 17). The heart settled in his wisdom delights our Father (v. 15). The heart is, of course, the whole person from the inner point of view: thought, desire, imagination, conscience, ambition. What we think, we are, says Proverbs.

Day 5: It Takes All Sorts! (Prov. 26:12–27)

What a collection of very believable people in Proverbs 26! The conceited person—why there's more hope for a thickhead (v. 12)! The idler/wastrel/work-shy for whom any excuse will do (v. 13), bed is always the preferred option (v. 14), any effort is too exhausting (v. 15)—but from his armchair vantage, how very judicious (v. 16). Meet the busybody (v. 17) and the inveterate "life and soul of the party" (vv. 18–19). Observe the tragic consequences of tittle-tattle and argumentativeness (vv. 20–22) and the hard gloss of earnestness and charm hiding evil and malice (vv. 23–26). But there is a justice that works its way out (vv. 26–27).

Day 6: In Praise of Diligence (Prov. 27:18–27)

Just as Proverbs has it in for the indolent, it loves the diligent and commends the diligent life (see week 1, day 3). Proverbs 27:18 is a typical mixture of sound advice and worldly wisdom—the way of prosperity and the way of promotion. But underneath it is the sound principle of living in God's world, not in man's. This is why the flocks (v. 23), new growth (v. 25), lambs and goats (v. 26), and milk (v. 27) are stressed. For your investments may let you down (v. 24), but your ground will not. Underneath its hardheaded approach, Proverbs is resting on divine promises (Gen. 8:22).

Day 7: Ignorance and Knowledge (Prov. 30:1–9)

The names given in Proverbs 30:1 are unknown, but from what he said, Agur was well qualified to be reckoned among the wise. First, he was content to live within the revelation God had given. There was much he did not know, and could not know until One came from heaven (John 3:12–13), but he knew that God had spoken, a pure and complete word, enabling us to trust and find refuge in him (Prov. 30:5–6). Second, he was content to commit the circumstances of his life to God, concerned only to maintain loyalty and to live according to what the Lord had revealed ("the name") of himself (vv. 7–9).

Week 3: You Have Heard of the Steadfastness of Job (James 5:11)

Day 1: God's Man and God's Mystery (Job 1:1–22)

Job comes before us as a man to whom God bore witness as blameless and upright (Job 1:8). This at once rules out the possibility that the suffering to come was provoked by sin. But what was its cause? We are never told. The Lord calls Satan's attention to Job (v. 8; cf. 2:3) and sets the limits on his liberty of action against Job (1:12; cf. 2:6), but he keeps to himself his reasons for doing so. The Lord does what pleases him in heaven and earth (Ps. 135:6; cf. 1 Sam. 3:18), and that's the end of it. But Satan is as much subject to his sovereignty as is Job. What a position of responsibility Job has, for unrevealed heavenly purposes depend on how he acts and reacts under stress.

Day 2: Why, Why, Why? (Job 3:11–26)

Job's friends have come to comfort him (Job 2:11–13), and with them he shares the blackness of his perplexity in five "whys" (3:11, 12, 16, 20, 23). If life is like this, why was he allowed to survive birth—indeed, why was he born at all? What is the point of life if it means only an unfulfilled longing for death? Why does God give life only to build impenetrable hedges around it? Questions are not in themselves wrong; they are part of our humanity, for God created us to want and need explanations. But questions more often deny God than affirm him, as Job did in verse 23. Even when it is at its most unacceptable and inexplicable, it is still the life God has apportioned to us.

Day 3: Let God Be God! (Job 9:1–13)

By this point two of Job's friends have spoken, and one is yet to speak. From different angles they have one explanation: sin in Job's life has brought him calamity. Job knows this is not true (and so do we), but one thing he knows for certain: God is God. He cannot be understood (Job 9:1–11), nor can he be called to account (vv. 12–13). Oddly, but for a reason we shall soon discover, this truth gives Job no rest. Yet it is the surest resting place of all in trouble. In his majestic wisdom and power the Sovereign of all creation knows what he is doing (vv. 4–10). Don't call him to account for his ways; accept and rest.

Day 4: Suffering and Certainty (Job 19:13–27)

Job saw the hand of God now in all things (Job 19:21)—the hand from which we can never be plucked (John 10:27–29). He also foresaw the fellowship of God then (Job 19:25–26) when all the testing is past. He is here with me now; I will be there with him then. He is "Redeemer" (v. 25), the Next of kin who takes all the trials, troubles, needs, inadequacies of his helpless relative as if they were his own and deals with them, himself paying every debt.

Day 5: Knowing Is No Comfort (Job 28:12–28)

If you have time, read the whole marvelous poem in Job 28. Man can search out almost everything (vv. 3, 9), but is there a mine for wisdom (v. 12)? Man is at a loss (v. 13); so is all creation (v. 14); money cannot buy it (vv. 15–19); searching upward or downward reveals nothing (vv. 21–22). God alone knows (vv. 23–27, see week 1, day 6), and we know only what he chooses to reveal (v. 28). But verse 28 is exactly how Job had lived (1:8)—and look where it brought him. Divine revelation is the only basis for life, but it brings no guarantee of ease or immunity.

Day 6: God—Wisdom, Justice, Power
(Job 38:31–35; 40:8–14; 41:15–19)

Job 38–39 drives home the measureless wisdom of God, exemplified in creation. In 40:8–14 the Lord (sarcastically) invites Job to undertake the moral government of the world, implying that only God can rule with perfect justice. Job 40:15–41:34 describes two terrifying, powerful monsters (40:15; 41:1), quite beyond man's power to master but subject to God. Job already knew all this about God—that he is endless in wisdom, absolute in justice, and sovereign in power—but not until the Lord himself came and said it to him (38:1) did the truth become his comfort, for he found himself in personal communion with an infinite God in whom he could rest. We have the voice of God in the Word of God.

Day 7: Home at Last (Job 42:1–16)

The end of Job's story (Job 42:1–16) is not just "happily ever after" sentimentality. The Lord proposed a fearful but limited test (Job 1–2); now that Job has passed the test, justice requires restoration. And after the manner of the Lord's gracious dealings, not just restoration but double. Even in the matter of children he has double—although the first family is gone to God. Well could James refer not only to Job's steadfastness but also to the Lord's ultimate outcome (James 5:11)—full of compassion indeed. See 2 Corinthians 4:16–5:1; Revelation 7:9–17.

Week 4: Living in a World That Does Not Add Up

Day 1: Nothing Is Going Anywhere! (Eccles. 1:2–11)

A hymn addresses God as "Eternal Ruler of the ceaseless round,"[2] and that is exactly what Ecclesiastes sees: human life (Eccles. 1:4), day and night (v. 5), climatic changes (v. 6), the constant cycling of water (v. 7)—and no matter how inquiry is pursued (v. 8), it all seems to add up to nothing (v. 9). As a general truth, nothing really novel appears (v. 10). Even the most dramatic scientific discoveries are only the uncovering of what has always been so. So what does it all mean—if anything? The eye looks out on "vanity" that does not add up.

Day 2: But God Is in Business! (Eccles. 2:24–3:22)

Even though to our eye life does not add up, there is satisfaction in it (Eccles. 2:24–25). There is a life of pleasing God, bringing blessing, and what's more, it is all going somewhere: to the final settlement when the meek shall inherit the earth (v. 26). The experiences that do not add up for me make sense to God, who

---

2. John W. Chadwick, "Eternal Ruler of the Ceaseless Round" (1864).

apportions all the contrasting experiences of life (3:1–8), adding beauty to everything in its time (v. 11). He wills our joy in the present (v. 12), moves to judgment in the future (v. 15), apportioning tests to bring us to a true self-awareness, lest we live purely animal lives (v. 18).

Day 3: Market Forces and Spiritual Bequests (Eccles. 5:10–20)

Typical of its sharp perceptiveness of life, Ecclesiastes turns its microscope on money, seen by people and governments alike as the great panacea—but is it? After all, experience shows that it does not in fact bring satisfaction (Eccles. 5:10–12), that it is highly vulnerable to change and chance (vv. 13–14), and that death cancels all bank balances (vv. 15–17). It is very different when life, joy in life, and heart satisfaction are all seen as God's gift (vv. 18–20).

Day 4: Living with an Unknown Future (Eccles. 8:2–9:1)

How oddly life works out (fails to add up) in respect of virtue and reward, crime and punishment. A person tries to live prudently within the given framework of society, but misery still weighs heavily (Eccles. 8:2–6). The only certain future is death (vv. 7–8). People hurtfully dominate each other (v. 9). The wicked cynically practice religion, and society praises them, which leads to social deterioration (vv. 10–11). Faith takes a different view of things (vv. 12–13), but the problem remains: moral rewards are reversed (v. 14). No one can make sense of life (vv. 16–17). So what is there to do? Rest in God's hands (9:1).

Day 5: The Thinking Life (Eccles. 9:17–10:7)

Ecclesiastes 9:13–16 asserts that wisdom is better than folly. Then 9:17–10:7 comments on that claim. Two different words are translated "fool/folly": in 9:17 and 10:2 the "fool" is the "thickhead," who cannot think straight even when he tries; in 10:1, 3, and 6 he is the "fathead," who lives without thinking. The way of wisdom is not easy—it meets with loud and effective opposition (9:17–18), and it can easily be spoiled (10:1). But it characterizes the properly constituted person (v. 2), faces life calmly (v. 4), yet by no means always or automatically succeeds (vv. 5–7). Uncomfortable—but realistic and all too true!

Day 6: Words and Work (Eccles. 10:12–20)

Ecclesiastes 9:7–10 advocates gusto in enjoying life. Then 10:12–20 explores this principle, first in the realm of speech. Gusto in talk is the sign of a fool (vv. 12–15) who, when it comes down to it, could not even tell you how to get to the town center. Besides, even the unspoken thought can get you into dire trouble (v. 20). Second is gusto in the realm of diligence: in government, the good things of life must be subordinate to the duties of life (vv. 16–17); privately, where there is idleness, there is no income to repair the roof (v. 18); enjoyment is all very well, but there must be a sound income to undergird needs (v. 19). All this too is realistic thinking.

Day 7: Conclusions (Eccles. 11:9–12:14)

Oh yes, life is for living (Eccles. 9:7–10), and not least when you are young (11:9). But there are other considerations too: judgment is coming (v. 9), and death is coming (12:1–7). Life is like day, always darkening toward night; like changeable weather, always coming on to rain (v. 2); like a great house falling into decay, its upkeep exceeding the strength of the residents (v. 3). Morning tasks ("grinding") are all that can be managed, so bolt the doors (v. 4). Sleep is broken by a sound as light as birdsong—even though hearing is not what it used to be. All sorts of things seem to be threats, and there is no longer a spring in the step; yes, death is on its way (vv. 5–8). Life does not add up—unless . . . unless there are words of truth (vv. 9–10), to stimulate ("goads"), to give security ("nails"), words from the Shepherd, God himself (v. 11). This is the real conclusion—to reverence and obey (v. 13).

———

OLD TESTAMENT REVELATION OF GOD
Meet the God of Whom the
Old Testament Speaks

Week 1: God the Creator

Day 1: Getting the Place Ready (Gen. 1:1–13)

The Bible insists that every bit of what we call "reality" ("the heavens and the earth," Gen. 1:1) began with God. Nothing originated itself; he originated it all. As for "without form and void" (v. 2), think of a sculptor sitting before a huge block of stone: at present it means nothing, but he knows how he will cut and shape it until it expresses his meaning. But of course, God also created that huge block of matter to begin with! The "Spirit of God" stands at hand ready to execute the will of God, and suddenly the all-creating Word is spoken. The mere expression of what God wants brings it into being. Since his workmanship is an expression of what he is himself, his first move is to fill the created universe with light.

Day 2: Ordering Life (Gen. 1:14–28)

The first three days of God's work match the second three (see fig. A.1).

Day 1	Light	**Day 4**	The ordered sequence of light, the great luminaries
Day 2	Sea and sky	**Day 5**	Sea and sky filled with life
Day 3	The habitable world	**Day 6**	The world's inhabitants

Figure A.1   The days of creation

Note the verb "to create." The Old Testament uses it only of God: it points to things that are so great or so novel that they require him as their cause. Everything began with God (Gen. 1:1); animate life came from the life-giving Creator (v. 21); humankind needed a threefold "created" (v. 27), being the crown of creation and the creature par excellence.

Day 3: Creator and King (Ps. 33:6–11)

Yes, it was as easy as that for the Creator—a word was enough (Ps. 33:6, 9). Think of the men and machines we need to widen a main road—what power, then, is this that simply says what is to happen? No wonder we are called to "stand in awe" (v. 8). But his power as Creator extends also into another sphere (v. 10), into the story of life on earth, history, the sphere of the plans of people and nations. Never think of the Creator simply as the One who pushed the boat out at the start and thereafter stands on the shore hoping for the best. He has the decisive word in what happens on earth, foiling humankind and implementing his own will (vv. 10–11). This does not mean we will understand what he is doing; it does mean we can live serenely and trustfully.

Day 4: "Thy Bountiful Care" (Ps. 104:1–3, 10–15)

It is not by chance that the same-sized earth annually produces more than enough for its growing brood. The sadness is that we allow ourselves to be baffled by the challenge of distributing the Creator's bounty equitably. But what a telling, moving picture of God we have in Psalm 104: the wild donkey (v. 11), birds nesting and perching (v. 12), soil awaiting rainfall (v. 13), domestic beasts (v. 14), humankind (v. 15)—all alike the objects of divine, tender loving care. This has been the truth about God from the start: remember the free abundance of the garden (Genesis 2)? His is an overflowing bounty, in the beginning unasked for—laid on, waiting for the first human pair—and now, because of our sinfulness, undeserved, but still there. Bountiful care indeed.

Day 5: Shared Strength (Isa. 40:25–31)

There are two ways of telling most stories. Astronomers can plot the heavens, describe the movement of stars, anticipate their rising and setting. Only the Bible can tell us why they are there in such reliable order—each one called by name (Isa. 40:26) and put in place by the faithful, mighty Creator God. Never look at the night sky and think of mechanical order and necessity. Look up and worship God: he does it. And because he is limitless and unwearying in power, everything is in place (v. 28). Learn a lesson with Isaiah: what the Creator reveals in creation he shares with us. The unfainting, unwearying God can make us like himself (v. 31).

Day 6: Special Creation, Special Care (Isa. 43:1–2)

The words "Jacob" and "Israel" (Isa. 43:1) in the Old Testament do not point to someone other than you and me; they point to the Lord's people, the "Israel of God" (Gal. 6:16), the descendants of Abraham (Rom. 4:11), the "circumcision" (Phil. 3:3). Just as the Lord created the world around us, so by the same exercise of his will and power he created us to be his people (Eph. 2:10). And just as he superintends the world he created (see day 5), so he lovingly superintends us, looking on us and saying, "You are mine" (Isa. 43:1). Life is not all grim, of course, but it is in the grim days (v. 2) that we need the special assurance that he is with us and that all is well. The Lord's people are his protected species.

Day 7: New Creation (Isa. 65:17–25)

Our sinful ways have sadly marred the beauty and proper functioning of the Lord's lovely creation. It is not enough to become "green" and environmentally aware. We need also to lament and repent. But ultimately, the Creator will not leave his workmanship to fail or languish. He will (one day, as we say) create all things anew—the environment (Isa. 65:17), people (v. 18), and experiences (v. 19). No more sadness (v. 19), no more curse

(v. 20; cf. Gen. 3:14–19), no more insecurity (Isa. 65:22), but fellowship with God (v. 24) and unity throughout his created order (v. 25).

Week 2: God the Revealer

Day 1: The God Who Speaks (Ex. 3:11–15)

We read it so familiarly, "God said to Moses," that we can forget what a unique marvel it is that God should speak to a human being. Specially privileged people like Moses were brought into a conversational relationship with the Lord—even arguing the toss with him! But from the beginning (e.g., Gen. 2:16; 17:1) the Lord's people on earth have been marked off by the fact that God spoke to them and that they have the Word of God to direct their lives. God has not kept silent, waiting for us to search for him. He has come out to us, telling us of himself, directing us by his Word. And he kept on speaking his Word until the full revelation of God was possessed on earth, our written Bibles. We are still the people of that Word.

Day 2: The Hunger of Natural Religion (Ps. 19:1–6)

Suppose God had never spoken—what would we know about him? The heavens do "declare" his glory and excite awe in us (Ps. 19:1). But which voice shall we heed—the sunset telling of beauty or the volcano telling of destruction? This is why Psalm 19:2 says that nature "pours out . . . knowledge," and yet verse 3 says, literally, "There is no speech or words; their voice is not heard." We look at nature and talk to ourselves about what we see. If that was all we had, we would remain hungry for a real, sure, unequivocal voice from heaven, a voice coming from outside ourselves, revealing to us the God we dimly sense, pulling together into one coherent revelation all the differing perceptions that come to us from the world around. Indeed, we must learn to glory in what he has created—and to hunger for the sure word that, in grace to us, he has spoken.

Day 3: The Joy of Knowing (Ps. 19:7–14)

Pick out the leading words in Psalm 19:7–9: in verse 7, "law" refers to "teaching," and "statutes" to "testimonies" (what the Lord has "testified" about himself); in verse 8, "precepts" refers to his detailed instructions for life, and "commandment" to authoritative orders; in verse 9, "ordinances" (NRSV; "rules," ESV) refers to his royal edicts, what he has "judged" to be right. He has not left us, you see, to fathom things out as best we can and hope to muddle through. He is a God who has spoken, and his people possess his Word—in our very privileged case, the complete Word, the Bible. We are called to respond with our emotions (v. 10), delighting in the sweetness of his Word; with mind and conscience (vv. 11–13), learning, obeying, sensitive to fault; and in will (v. 14), committing ourselves to what pleases him.

Day 4: Through Chosen People (1 Sam. 3:19–4:1)

The Lord's word came *to* and *through* Samuel. This simple story in 1 Samuel 3:19–4:1 illustrates the Lord's way of doing things. He does not write his word in mile-high letters across the sky; he chooses people to whom and then through whom he proposes to speak. We usually call them prophets in the Old Testament and apostles in the New. Hebrews 1:1–2 outlines the process from beginning to end: the days of prophet after prophet, each of whom brought from God his own facet of divine truth, a bit here, a bit there, now by this method, now by that. But the whole diamond, in all its facets, shone with full brilliance only when the Son of God, our Lord Jesus Christ, came to us, validating all that had gone before, assuring us that we can trust the Word of God.

Day 5: The Renewing Word (Ps. 119:153–160)

For the ESV "give" in Psalm 119:154, 156, 159, read "renew." The psalmist is enduring suffering (v. 153) and foes who persecute

(v. 157). His reaction is (1) to hold the Lord's "law" ("teaching," v. 153) in his mind, (2) to obey the Lord's "statutes" (what the Lord has testified about himself, v. 157) in his life, and (3) to love the Lord's "precepts" (his detailed requirements, v. 159) with his emotions. Life's fortunes change, but the word the Lord has spoken ("your word," v. 160) is eternal truth and an unchanging basis for living. But also the Lord who promises renewal (v. 154) and whose love guarantees that he will give us new life as we need it (v. 159) actually gives us that life as we live by his laws (v. 156; cf. Acts 5:32).

Day 6: Wisdom in Life's Conundrums (Dan. 2:17–23)

Daniel found his God to be a God of revelation at a time of personal crisis. Reading between the lines, we guess that King Nebuchadnezzar wearied of the pretensions of his "wise men" and, when he needed an interpretation, put them deliberately on the spot by requiring them to tell both the dream and its meaning, on pain of death. Daniel banded himself with his friends into a fellowship of prayer (Dan. 2:17–18) and proved that his God is one "who reveal[s]" (v. 23 NRSV). While we would be foolish to expect or depend on anything as chancy as a dream, we would be equally foolish not to commit our problems to God in earnest prayer, to share our concerns with trusted friends, and to expect God to open his Word to us for our guidance.

Day 7: The Ultimate Vision (Isa. 33:17–24)

The New Testament (e.g., Heb. 12:22; Rev. 21:1–4) teaches us that "Zion" (Isa. 33:20) is a picture of the heavenly blessings we now enjoy in Christ and of the future that awaits us. Isaiah sees it as a place of secure tenure (v. 20), unruffled peace (v. 21), the solution to all the inadequacies and failures of life (v. 23), a place of personal fulfillment and the forgiveness of sins (v. 24). But above all, the vision of the Lord, the King (v. 17), ever present and saving.

Week 3: God the Covenant Maker

Day 1: A Great Promise Made Certain (Gen. 9:8–17)

In the Bible, "covenant" is used for very special promises that the Lord made. Like all covenant promises, his promise to Noah comes on the sole initiative of God. Noah neither asked for it nor expected it; God was not obliged to make it. He promised because he wanted to promise: "never again" (Gen. 9:11, 15). The "sign of the covenant" (vv. 12, 17) gives visible expression to the promise. Imagine, whenever storm clouds gathered and everything reminded him of the way the great flood had come, Noah's relief at seeing the rainbow. He would say, "But God has promised." Baptism and the Lord's Supper are today's covenant signs confirming to us all God's promises in Christ.

Day 2: More Promises: Parents and Their Children (Gen. 17:1–10)

The Bible is full of the promises of God: he loves making promises. To Abram the promise was (1) personal (Gen. 17:5): he would become a new man with new powers; (2) domestic (v. 6): this is the sort of family he would have; (3) spiritual (v. 7): the Lord committed himself to Abram and his descendants; and (4) territorial (v. 8): God would give a land to live in. Next, the Lord wrapped up his promise in a sign that is to be applied to Abraham, the adult believer, and to his eight-day-old sons (vv. 9–12). How very precious that God extends his promises to our children (Acts 2:39).

Day 3: God Means His Promises: Have Patience (Ex. 6:1–8)

Moses was in a deep trough of depression in Exodus 6. He had been sent by God to bring Israel out of Egypt, but everything had gone wrong (actually through Moses's own disobedience and mishandling of the situation). But the Lord was not knocked off course. He had made his promises long ago to Abraham, and he had no intention of failing to keep them. We may fail, but he does not. What he has promised he will most certainly keep and perform. We get impatient: why has nothing happened? Why has God done nothing? But his timetable is not ours. He will keep his promises, never fear. "Trust and obey." Be patient.

Day 4: Another Side to the Covenant (Ps. 89:1–8)

When the Lord's people first asked him to give them a king, it was indeed a lapse of real trust on their part. They wanted the security of a permanent institution instead of the "strain" of simply trusting the Lord when dangers arose. But the Lord took their second best and made it his first best, covenanting to David that he would have unending kingship—and ultimately that the perfect King would reign in David's line (Luke 1:30–33). In this way God's central covenant promises came to be focused on the expected King, and we know that, in fact, all God's promises have come to fulfillment in the Lord Jesus Christ (2 Cor. 1:20). Psalm 89 is a product of a time when God did not seem to keep his promises: its message is that at such a time, far from doubting the promises, we should turn them into prayer and wait for God to keep them.

Day 5: The Coming Covenant (1): Like a
True Marriage—Peace (Isa. 54:5–10)

The prophets took the idea of the covenant and allowed it to shape their vision of the future. Outside this covenant, life is like all the stress and trauma of a broken marriage (Isa. 54:6), or like being caught up in the great flood (v. 9). But Isaiah foresees a covenanted (i.e., pledged, guaranteed) peace (v. 10). The peace he speaks of is, in the first instance, peace with God, as in 53:5, secured for us by the sin-bearing work of the Lord's Servant, our Lord Jesus Christ. Much of Isaiah's vision awaits fulfillment. We have peace with God (Rom. 5:1), but the fruition of unbroken peace awaits the coming of Christ.

Day 6: The Coming Covenant (2): Sin Forgiven and Forgotten (Jer. 31:31–34)

Jeremiah saw that the Lord would yet covenant a cluster of good things: (1) a new heart, shaped so as to obey God's law (Jer. 31:33); (2) a direct knowledge of the Lord, "knowing" him person to person, intimately, lovingly (v. 34); and (3) all this arising from (note "for" at the end of v. 34) sin being forgiven and forgotten. Isaiah told us that this dealing with sin would be the work of the Lord's Servant (Isaiah 53); Jeremiah does not go into detail but leaves us to wonder at the result: the Lord has not only forgiven our sins, he has forgotten we ever committed them.

Day 7: The Coming Covenant (3): God Dwelling among His People (Ezek. 37:24–28)

See how Ezekiel summarizes what Isaiah and Jeremiah said: like Jeremiah, he foresaw the days of the new covenant as marked by obedience (Ezek. 37:24). Like Isaiah, he foresaw a covenant of peace (v. 26). Like Psalm 89, he foresaw a coming David (Ezek. 37:24). But he climaxed his vision with the thought of the Lord dwelling among his people—his perpetual and unchanging presence through an everlasting covenant promise (v. 26).

Week 4: God the Redeemer
Day 1: The Kinsman-Redeemer (Ruth 4:1–10)

The story of Boaz and Ruth (of which we have read here in chapter 4 only the climax—why not read the whole book?) illustrates a beautiful Old Testament provision. When people got into difficulties they could not handle—a debt or the necessity to sell home or land—their next of kin had the right to step in and make the whole burden his own, and they had the right to expect him to do so. This is what Boaz did for Naomi and Ruth: he made their difficulties his own and then solved and ended them. This is one way in which, by the laws he gave them, the Lord was teaching his people to be like himself: for he is himself our Next of kin, our Kinsman-Redeemer.

Day 2: The Lord Is Like That Too! (Gen. 48:10–16)

Genesis 48:16 is the first time the verb "to redeem" occurs in the Bible. Jacob is approaching the end of his long, varied life. Looking back, he sees one golden thread running through it all: God has been his Shepherd; the Lord's "angel" (an Old Testament preview of the Lord Jesus) has been his Kinsman-Redeemer, his Next of kin. In all his experiences and scrapes, Jacob has never been alone; there has always been a divine "relative" identifying with him, sharing and bearing his burdens. This was the blessing Jacob sought for the sons of Joseph as he blessed them. It is our blessing too: a Shepherd to lead and care, a Kinsman-Redeemer to take on himself every disaster that would threaten to overwhelm us.

Day 3: The Great Redemption (1): In the Past (Isa. 63:7–9)

The whole passage of Isaiah 63:7–14 makes it clear that Isaiah is looking back to the exodus, to the Lord's work of grace and power in bringing our ancestors out of Egyptian bondage and death. Verse 7 speaks of the Lord's ever-unfailing love and of his "compassion," his heart-throbbing affection for his people—all of which led him to become their "Savior" (v. 8). In verse 9 we read how he identified with them in every sorrow and carried them through all their hardships in the wilderness journey. At the heart of it all is the key idea: love and pity made him their Redeemer, their Next of kin, their divine burden bearer.

Day 4: The Great Redemption (2): In the Future (Isaiah 35)

Even for Isaiah, chapter 35 exemplifies a literary and lyrical high spot as he strains forward to see a divinely transformed people with every weakness healed (vv. 5–6), in a new environment (v. 7) where every need is met. The picture of the future is drawn from the exodus of the past: a holy people on the journey home, guarded alike from their own frailty within and from every threat from outside (vv. 8–9). They are on their way back to Zion (see week 2, day 7)—and they are the Lord's "redeemed" (v. 9). Their Kinsman-Redeemer has led them all their life through (as for Jacob, see day 2), and now he is bringing them safely home to glory.

Day 5: Plentiful Redemption (Psalm 130)

The word translated in Isaiah 35:10 as "ransom" (NKJV) is a different word from the "kinsman-redeemer" word. This same Hebrew word occurs in Psalm 130:7–8 but is translated "redemption" and "redeem" there (ESV); "ransom" is a better translation because the word focuses more on the price that has been paid (as when ransoms are paid today) than on the person (the kinsman) who does the paying. This too is part of the Lord's ever-unfailing love (v. 7). Psalm 130 is concerned with sin (vv. 1–3), in respect of which we need "mercy" (or grace, v. 2) and "forgiveness" (v. 4). But at a price. Sin cannot be overlooked or swept under the carpet. The holy law of the holy God requires a price to be paid. If he truly is our Kinsman-Redeemer, we would expect him to pay it—which is exactly what he did in the Old Testament sacrifices and, finally and fully, in the Lord Jesus Christ (Heb. 10:12).

Day 6: "That Will Cover It" (Lev. 17:10–11)

"Blood" is very important in the Bible—for the reason given in Leviticus 17:10–11. It is the life. We speak of "lifeblood," because we know that loss of blood means loss of life. In this way, in the Bible, blood was the symbol of life ended in death. In verse 11 "atonement" means "covering price": we hand over money for a debt or a purchase, and we say, "That will cover it"—that is, remove it by paying for it completely. In the Old Testament, animal sacrifices "cover" sin debts, and in the New Testament, the final sacrifice of Jesus "covers" the whole debt of our sin—removes it out of God's sight and out of God's mind by paying it in full.

Day 7: The Blessing and Joy of Redemption (Isa. 44:21–23)

The "kinsman-redeemer" verb, used twice in Isaiah 44:22–23, is used in the Old Testament as a summary for all the redemption words. Our great Next of kin takes our debt as his own and pays the price on our behalf, settling it completely. Our sins, considered as an offense to God, incurring the penalty of his law, are totally gone—as completely as a cloud or mist evaporates under the heat of the sun (v. 22). "Transgressions" (v. 22) are "rebellions," sins of the will, our deliberate refusal of the Lord and his way, our determination to have our own way. "Sins" (v. 22) are actual, recordable wrongdoings of thought, word, and deed. Thus both inwardly (in person and will) and outwardly (in act and conduct), our sin has been dealt with—and to God's satisfaction, for he performed the work himself as our Next of kin.

GENERAL INDEX

SCRIPTURE INDEX